Sex

in the
Museum

Sex

in the
Museum

〉→◆ ◆←〈

My Unlikely Career at New York's
Most Provocative Museum

Sarah Forbes

St. Martin's Press   New York

www.stmartins.com

Designed by Meryl Sussman Levavi

Library of Congress Cataloging-in-Publication Data

Names: Forbes, Sarah, 1982– author.
Title: Sex in the museum : my unlikely career at New York's most
    provocative museum / Sarah Forbes.
Description: First edition. | New York : St. Martin's Press, [2016]
Identifiers: LCCN 2015038926| ISBN 9781250041678 (hardcover) |
    ISBN 9781466838574 (e-book)
Subjects: LCSH: Forbes, Sarah. | Museum of Sex (New York, N.Y.) |
    Museum Curators—New York (State)—New York. | Sex—History—
    Museums. | Sex Customs—History—Exhibitions. | Sexology.
Classification: LCC HQ12 .F65 2016 | DDC 392.6—dc23
LC record available at http://lccn.loc.gov/2015038926

Our books may be purchased in bulk for promotional, educational, or
business use. Please contact your local bookseller or the Macmillan
Corporate and Premium Sales Department at 1-800-221-7945, extension
5442, or by e-mail at MacmillanSpecialMarkets@macmillan.com.

First Edition: April 2016

10 9 8 7 6 5 4 3 2 1

For Forbedo, Kai, Zia, K. J. Lady, G. Duck, and the Count

Sex

in the
Museum

one

Please Don't Touch, Lick, Stroke, or Mount the Exhibits

On my desk I have a stack of books, a laptop, a phone charger, and an assortment of pens. I also have a butt plug, a masturbation sleeve, a mysterious menstruation tonic, and, of course, a pile of porn.

Welcome to the Museum of Sex.

People always ask me what a typical day at the office is like. It's hard to say because, really, no day is typical. I do, however, spend a lot of time on research, trying to keep ahead of all the sex-related stories that are constantly breaking. And every day I find something that makes me shout out to my coworkers, "Did you know . . . ?"

For example:

Did you know that people have inserted into their rectums items as diverse as lightbulbs, curling irons, ax handles, and seventy-two individual half-inch jeweler's saws?

Did you know that the word *vanilla* comes from the Latin word for *vagina* ("sheath") because at some point in history someone saw a resemblance to the vanilla bean?

Did you know that koala bears as a species have rampant chlamydia?

Did you know that according to some folk-medicine love charms, the best way to keep a man faithful is to urinate in his morning coffee?

As curator of the Museum of Sex, I know something is exhibition-worthy when it makes me stop and wonder. For most people, the simple fact that the museum exists gives them pause.

I get it. There was a time, though it's getting hard to remember, when I had my own *what the?* moment. Most of us are lucky if we grow up with an art gallery, a science museum, maybe a natural history museum. But a sex museum?

Institutions like MoSex (the museum's pet name) aren't the stuff of elementary school field trips. Most of us don't have a frame of reference for something like this, and our long-standing assumptions confuse us. Museums are highbrow; sex is base. Museums are public; sex is private. The two just don't go together. No wonder people are wary when they walk through our doors. Will they see live girls? Will there be rooms to have sex? Can they masturbate while they watch the films? Come naked?

The answer, disappointing to some, is a categorical "no." The Museum of Sex is just like any other cultural institution: a haven for art, artifacts, and ephemera. After all, the word *museum* is in our title for a reason. It's just that, in our case, we are dedicated to the "history, evolution, and cultural significance of human sexuality." In other words—sex.

Yes, we have a sign that says, "Please don't touch, lick, stroke, or mount the exhibits." And, yes, our guards often have to remind patrons, "That sex machine on display is not for you to use, ma'am." Or, "Sir, please get off the St. Andrew's Cross" (a seven-foot brushed-steel X, once the main restriction apparatus in Domina M's dungeon). But that's just the price of doing business when you feature the world's most fascinating topic.

Unlike many museums, we do allow photography. Our guards watch as thousands photo bomb themselves with the installations, in many cases trying to make it look as if they are engaged in the sexual act on display. I can't count the number of times our life-size sculpture of pandas coupling has been taken from behind for an interspecies Instagram. And for every penis that has graced our galleries, I'm confident a photo of someone pretending to fellate it exists on the Internet.

To more constructively channel this energy, we provide opportunities throughout the museum where people are encouraged to touch the exhibits. The torsos of a male and female RealDoll are long-standing interactives that give visitors a chance to experience the incredibly high-grade silicone of these exceptionally expensive, fully customizable sex dolls. Patrons viewing this installation can stick their hands into Plexiglas openings and feel the breasts, vulva, and penis of the dolls. Freedom does have its limits, though. During one of our exhibition parties someone bit the nipple off the female RealDoll. We learned our lesson. Now, anything fragile is dutifully kept under glass.

Here's an observation: although people eagerly squeeze the breasts and stick their fingers into the vagina of the female doll, fewer confidently grab the shaft of the male's penis. Could it be that, even in a museum, our society thinks women's bodies are fair game? Are there social taboos that prevent patrons from touching a male penis—women who worry they might be "slut shamed" for a public demonstration of sexuality; heterosexual men concerned with doing anything that would deviate from ideas of "straight" masculinity? After more than a decade working at the Museum of Sex, it's questions like these that keep me fascinated.

But we do like to keep our visitors engaged, which is why we offer a wide array of inviting displays. Like the Fuck Bike #001, created by Andrew H. Shirley and William Thomas Porter, which we had once positioned in our shop window to entice both exhibitionists and voyeurs alike. Created from multiple spokes, wheels, rods, and bike parts, this eleven-foot-long sculptural piece can be mounted like any normal bike. Yet in this case, the act of peddling causes a flesh-colored, veiny dildo to flop back and forth horizontally, transforming it—quite literally—into a bike that can fuck. And yes, it's a highly popular interactive.

Jump for Joy is also a favorite. A bouncy castle made of gigantic breasts, this immersive installation encourages people to leap into the air and throw themselves off enormous inflated latex mammaries (designed to reflect the diversity of shape, color, and size that exists in reality). And they do. With big smiles on their faces, patrons will quite literally jump for joy—a once-in-a-lifetime experience that overcomes any initial embarrassment. It's fun to watch people enjoying themselves and being carefree, not exactly what we tend to associate with most museum experiences. And as the Huffington Post says, "If This Boob Bounce House Doesn't Turn You On to Art, We Don't Know What Will."

Most people come to MoSex looking for something to shock

them. This was an easier feat when the museum opened a decade ago. Now, in the age of the Internet, it's becoming increasingly difficult to curate an entirely unique experience. What was once considered fringe is now considered (almost) mainstream. Depending on the audience, that is. Ten years ago, for example, few people knew the meaning of the term *bukkake*. Today I'm confident the average eighteen-year-old would be able to provide a succinct definition: an act that involves multiple men ejaculating on an individual, typically on the face. (Also, a type of udon noodle.)

As curator, it's my job to create exhibitions, turning shocking concepts and images into something that leaves people with a greater understanding—or at least broader thinking—of sexuality. That potential shift in the way people view the vast, amazing, and often unbelievable arena of sexuality is what makes me love my job. Before working at the Museum of Sex I would never have known that early condoms or "rubbers" were reused multiple times, were as thick as bicycle tires, and smelled of sulfur. Nor would I be able to quote "grannies," "upskirt," "nip slip," and "facesitting" as the twentieth, forty-sixth, sixty-fifth, and eighty-third most popular Internet porn searches. What a difference a decade makes.

→◆ ◆←

It was my summer of fun before diving into real life. I would soon be starting grad school at the New School for Social Research—advanced courses in anthropology with a focus on gender. The plan was to become a super anthropology nerd, do the academia thing, live with an indigenous tribe somewhere to earn my Ph.D. and become a professor, fully qualified to teach those fresh faces in Anthropology 101. In the meantime, I was working as a promotional model in the mornings and a nanny in the afternoons. At night, I was a highly proficient party girl and could usually be found downtown at Le Souk at three a.m.

But every anthropology nerd needs a home base, so I teamed up with a college friend to find an apartment. Nora enlisted a broker named Avi, a tall, dark, and handsome Israeli who seemed more interested in flirting than finding us a place to live. It would have been harmless fun if it weren't for the fact that my mother, who joined us for some of the apartment hunting, was ready to do some serious matchmaking. But despite his good looks and my mother's not-so-subtle seal of approval, it just wasn't going to happen. I had a boyfriend. A long-distance boyfriend, but a boyfriend nonetheless.

A week into our apartment hunt, after Nora and I viewed a string of nearly uninhabitable places (the type so small you'd have to choose between peeing sitting down and closing the bathroom door), Avi found us a loft. It was on the corner of Twenty-sixth and Lexington, right near the line between Gramercy and Little India. Turn north, you'd come across small Indian restaurants and sari shops. East, and you'd find the frat boy bars on Third Avenue. For a budding anthropologist, it was the perfect observation ground. The apartment really was something special. It had tremendous windows that framed the gold-roofed New York Life Building by day and the lights of the Empire State Building by night. But how could it be in our price range?

"I really negotiated this down for you," Avi told me.

I believed him. And I wasn't entirely surprised when he asked me out to lunch. Maybe it was naive of me, but I like to believe that, sometimes, lunch means just lunch. Or so I thought until he said he'd like me to meet his mother. I put down my sandwich, half-eaten.

"You want to introduce me to your mother?"

"Yes. She's coming from Israel next week. You should meet her."

"You want me to meet your mother?" I repeated.

"Yes," he said, with intensity. "I do."

I knew that was my cue to tell him about my boyfriend, Nick—but would it also mean the end of the apartment? I didn't agree to meet his mother—I'm not totally unscrupulous—but Manhattan real estate is a tough nut to crack, so I decided not to volunteer any more information than was absolutely necessary.

This proved tricky when the loft came through and Nick happened to be visiting the weekend I had to sign the lease.

"I can go with you," he said.

I hesitated. The deal wasn't solid until the rental papers were signed.

"It's probably best if you don't come," I said.

"You don't want me to?"

"It's not that I don't want you to, it's just that the broker is getting us a crazy good deal on this place and I feel like. . . ." I stammered.

"What, like he's doing it because he's interested in you?"

I nodded.

"Sarah," Nick said, shaking his head.

"What? I didn't encourage him. I just didn't—" The whole incident had become a case study in third-wave feminism.

Nick laughed and threw up his hands in resignation. "Fine. I'll find some way to occupy myself while you lock in your shady rent deal."

So while I signed the paperwork with Avi and Nora, Nick killed time walking around the neighborhood.

I called him when the deal was sealed. "It's all signed!" I said, barely able to contain my excitement. "I officially have my own apartment! Let's celebrate. Where are you?"

"Some place called the Museum of Sex."

"The Museum of *what*?"

"You heard me," he said. "The Museum of Sex."

"Um . . . do you want me to come meet you?" I asked. "And will I be cool with this place?"

"It's just a room full of weird art. Girls peeing. Photos of sex parties. Nothing that interesting." I could hear his sneakers squeaking against the steps as he explored. "Actually you might like this. It's called *Sex Among the Lotus: 3,000 Years of Chinese Erotic Obsession.*"

That was all it took. Within five minutes I had arrived at a nondescript building on Twenty-seventh Street, just off Fifth Avenue. I paid for my little red ticket, not realizing it would be the ticket to the next ten years of my life.

Inside the entranceway, the walls were painted red, with chipping paint and neon-red lights. Directly in front of me were heavy steel doors, and beyond that a gift shop filled with sex-related souvenirs. I took a left through a small passageway to the first floor and an exhibition called *Get Off*. It featured ads, cartoons, and drawings by Lynda Benglis, AA Bronson, Tee Corinne, and Jeff Koons, postwar artists who use sexual titillation to provoke responses from their viewers.

I spotted Nick at the end of the gallery. "I'm glad you've spent your afternoon watching porn. Is this to get back at me for not telling the broker about you?" I teased.

He smiled and shrugged his shoulders. "It's not my fault you decided to get an apartment around the corner from the Museum of Sex."

With his arm around the small of my back, Nick and I explored the beautiful, dimly lit exhibition *Sex Among the Lotus*. We saw ancient erotic ceramics, actual preserved bound feet on loan from the Mütter Museum, and contemporary Chinese porn, all set in spotlit red lacquered alcoves.

I was surprised at how much the exhibition drew me in. I'd never been to a museum that discussed sexual positions or showed illustrated sex guides used to educate Chinese brides for their wedding nights. I certainly had never seen objects used to decorate and penetrate genitalia.

It was safe to say I'd never think of the word *museum* in the same way again.

"Why don't you see if they're hiring," Nick suggested. "Talk to the guy at the front desk."

"Very funny," I said.

Despite my fascination with anthropology, I had no desire to work in a museum. I guess I've always considered museums— traditional museums, that is—to be somewhat disingenuous. Of course they can serve as institutions of education and research, but they're still influenced by an unfortunate legacy, one that often presents itself as an authority on a particular people (indigenous groups, let's say), yet are not inclusive of those communities. For instance, several years into the twenty-first century, the American Museum of Natural History featured a diorama of a Middle Eastern souk (bazaar) with a figure on a magic carpet flying proudly over the marketplace. Not exactly accurate academia in a post-9/11 world.

And then there are the many Native American tribes actively fighting to have their ancestors' bodies repatriated. It's shameful, really, that in 2016 people and their cultures are still treated as specimens to be displayed in glass cases, often without proper context and appreciation. Old habits really do die hard, I suppose. The legacy of today's museums can be traced back to the Renaissance, when the world's artifacts and treasures were amassed by wealthy collectors—often by ill-begotten means. Traveling the world and collecting treasures was today's equivalent of having a black American Express card or a rare sports car. Through purchase and theft, the artifacts of other lands became the booty that fill many museum's collections. This dirty little secret of the museum world is the reason why I never thought I'd be working in one. But then, I'd never imagined a museum of sex.

two

Museum of Sex Normal

I blew off Nick's suggestion to apply for a job at the Museum of Sex. Growing up in a family where spending money had to be earned, babysitting had been my go-to profession since I was a teenager. Now, in the financially unpredictable postcollege period, I was grateful that I could support myself this way. I had been hired by a music-industry power couple who lived on Gramercy Park (with keys to the exclusive secret garden), and who were excited that they found a young educated woman who could also teach their little one some Spanish. Instead of the experience being a chapter out of *The Nanny Diaries,* the family was tremendously laid back. I really enjoyed the little girl I was looking after. Nevertheless, I couldn't help thinking that I should get a job that would make use of my degree. I mean, if I was going to spend the next twenty years paying off student loans, it made sense to be doing something in the field, something that would actually fulfill my fascination with anthropology.

I came by it honestly, this captivation with anthropology. As a multiethnic child, raised between the hippie Four Corners of the Southwest and the affluence of Manhattan, it was my diverse background that fueled my interest in a discipline that would encourage me to explore the world. As my freshman-year anthropology professor, Professor Burton, liked to say, "People are drawn to anthropology because they feel some sort of dissatisfaction with their own society." For me, it wasn't dissatisfaction as much as I so often felt betwixt and between two worlds—in the "liminal stage" of multiple identities, an anthropologist might say.

I grew up in a nontraditional family structure. My parents divorced when I was three. My mother's fear of my father's drinking prompted her to petition the courts, at which point my father's parental rights were terminated.

My grandparents were a lifeline during this harrowing time (both emotionally and financially), especially Grandpa Marvin, with whom I had a special bond. Though three thousand miles away, Grandpa Marvin and I shared a nightly routine of a glass of chocolate milk and a chat, a long-distance call in which he would impersonate *Sesame Street* characters and encourage me to tell "Bert and Ernie" if anything was upsetting me. As a small child, and really, for the rest of my life, Grandpa was my sanctuary and my rock.

My mom, keen to start a new life, decided to separate from our previous identity, changing our names from Escobedo to Jacobs. It was all for the best, she told me. This new name, she said, would protect me from a father she said might kidnap me some drunken night. I've come to realize that was, in some respects, more drama than reality. But it was also about creating a new identity, one where I would no longer be labeled a "White Mexican."

It's not that "White Mexican" is a common category—far from it. It's just that when I was born in 1982, in the mountains of Arizona, to a fair freckly woman with red hair and a man with dark hair, eyes, and skin, the hospital officials simply couldn't grasp which category to put me in. What box to check. Although Mexicans are still heavily discriminated against in many parts of the country, I was differentiated by not being one thing or the other.

My mother's parents were descendants of Eastern European Jewish immigrants. My grandmother was forged from the worst of the Depression era, a child of immigrant sensibilities passionate to move beyond the confines of the New York Jewish ghetto. She was a daring woman, a tall blonde who worked hard and used her beauty and sense of style to escape poverty.

She met my grandfather at age sixteen when she crashed a frat party at NYU. The aspiring model-artist married the businessman, and they moved to the suburbs. (This was in the 1950s, when Long Island was considered "America's Frontier.") By the 1970s my grandfather's entrepreneurial efforts were paying off financially—his claim to fame being the fiberglass company that helped craft the Blue Whale that now hangs at the American Museum of Natural History. My mother was a bit indulged by this new wealth. Only twelve at the time of Woodstock, she would have been the perfect "trustafarian" flower child had she been born only been a decade earlier. Beautiful but insecure, extraordinarily book smart but not always street smart, my mother went off to Arizona at age sixteen to begin college. It was in Arizona that she met my dad, a Saudi sheik whose immense wealth came from oil. Well, that's what he told her on one of their first meetings. In reality, he was a humble Mexican American from a tiny mining town called Miami, Arizona. What started out as friendship evolved into a casual relationship, conducted mostly through letters while he was in the marines. After a brief time, my mom—impulsive, caught up in the idea of romance—accepted my father's proposal.

But with one legal document, I was no longer Sarah Escobedo, that White Mexican from Arizona. I was Sarah Jacobs, the Jewish girl on the Upper East Side of Manhattan.

Years later, it would be anthropology that would help me knit together my heritage. During my second year of college, I spent a semester in an anthropology and archaeology program in Mexico, where I ended up volunteering at a bright and cheery orphanage that was woefully understaffed. Aside from the intense experience of caring for dozens of babies, ranging in age from newborn to three, I was able to hone and direct my sociological interest.

The children of Casa del Sol were given up for many reasons, but what struck me most were the mothers, too poor to feed another mouth, who came to say farewell to children they would never see again and in many cases didn't want to give up. These mothers, many of whom were part of disenfranchised indigenous communities, had little control over their reproductive destinies. Access to contraceptives, contraceptive information, or even the power to decide when, how often, and with whom to sexually engage are sadly not rights afforded to every woman. In the disempowerment I witnessed at Casa del Sol, I could see the real-life struggles of inequality that were the discourse of my studies. This was no textbook or seminar. Here, in front of me, were tremendous hardship and sorrow. Sex was no longer just an act; its implications were knit into much larger dialogues. I would later understand these connections to be the backbone of much more sophisticated conversations, but they were revelations for me, then a sophomore in college.

My time in Mexico and my experiences at Casa del Sol changed me. I decided to dedicate the next two years of my life to the study of gender, race, and social structures. With this new momentum and incentive, I directed the rest of my undergraduate studies to the broad topic of gender.

And now, in my first year in New York, I had stumbled upon a place, a cultural institution, solely dedicated to looking at sex and gender. What was I waiting for?

→◆ ◆←

I handed my résumé to the guy behind the front desk—the same guy who'd sold me a ticket a month earlier. I didn't even ask if they were hiring, or specify what type of position I wanted. Professional, right?

I never really expected a call back.

A few weeks later, Nick and I were visiting his parents in New Jersey. We sat in the backyard as I hand painted one of his surfboards. This was all part of another one of my plans to set up a surf design company, move to Hawaii, and live out a Jack Johnson song after grad school. I'd fallen in love with the islands after a semester (almost) abroad. And why not keep my options open?

Then my phone rang.

It was the museum. Could I come in for an interview?

At age twenty-two, having never watched porn, visited a strip club, or owned a vibrator, I had an interview at the Museum of Sex.

It was a sweltering August day when I returned to the museum.

I had no idea what to wear. I decided on fitted white pants with thin beige pinstripes, a black knit tank top, and my usual assortment of accessories—my favorite part of getting dressed. By the time I walked the few blocks from my apartment to the corner of Twenty-seventh and Fifth Avenue, I was overheated and shiny.

Whereas most museums in New York City are grouped together on Museum Mile, a prestigious stretch of land from Eighty-second to 105th Street on the Upper East Side, the Museum of Sex lives in a crossroads for tourists visiting the Empire State and Flatiron Buildings. When the museum first opened in 2002, this was a less-than-desirable part of the city. It was within blocks of the drug-riddled Madison Square Park and the wholesale district, where Gucci-esque purses and jumbo packs of sweat socks are sold in bulk. In those days, you wouldn't just stumble upon the Museum of Sex—it had to be your destination. Dan, the museum's founder, chose that neighborhood because he knew that, in order for the museum to sustain itself financially, he would have to own the building that housed it.

But since that time, the area—along with much of New York— has undergone a gentrification. Danny Meyer's famous Shake Shack launched a revitalization of Madison Square Park, vastly transforming the area and its demographic. Mario Batali's Eataly has anchored the corner of Fifth Avenue and Twenty-third Street, and the Museum of Mathematics just moved in around the corner. There goes the neighborhood.

Pushing the buzzer for the museum's office, I had one last minute to pull myself together. I was nervous, mostly because I didn't really know what to expect. I had some sense of the standard interview questions: What are your greatest strengths? Describe a difficult work situation and what you did to overcome it. Where do you see yourself in five years? But even though I was interviewing at the Museum of Sex, the sex aspect didn't actually cross my mind. If I'd been asked, I almost certainly would have nodded my head, asserting I was "totally comfortable" with whatever the museum would throw at me. But really, I had no idea what I was in for.

"Hey, Sarah! Hot out there, right?" Ryan was the museum's anthropologist and researcher. He was in his late twenties, tall and skinny—an academic Luke Perry. My application came at a serendipitous time because he was on the verge of leaving to do fieldwork for his dissertation.

To get your Ph.D. in anthropology you need to do fieldwork, that is to say, conduct research and collect information outside of an academic setting. (It's one of the rare Ph.D.s that work that way.) Ryan was about to fulfill that part of his degree requirement. If he liked me, I would be his replacement while he was on leave from the museum. Although I was just starting grad school, I had spent the previous summer in Venezuela working for a think tank concerned with the violence and corruption rampant under President Chavez. I knew I had a lot to learn, but at least I had some solid research experience under my belt.

"Let me give you the official tour," Ryan said.

First up, *Get Off: Exploring the Pleasure Principle,* where I was greeted by an anthropomorphized vagina, with pasted-on googly eyes, smoking a cigarette. The projection was so large you could see every detail of her labia, every shaved follicle. Next was a monitor of the "pee videos" by artists Laurel Nakadate and Dora Malech. In the center of the gallery was a fluorescent sex furniture installation known as the *Karimsutra* (a play on the name of famous designer Karim Rashid), large enough for a group of a dozen people to enjoy in a wide range of positions.

I tried to appear nonchalant.

Upstairs, the office was filled with mismatched furniture, like a postcollege apartment decorated with hand-me-downs. It would be an understatement to say that the space was a little rough around the edges.

"This is our fully stocked liquor cabinet," he said, pointing to his right. "Sometimes you need a drink working here."

I was about to learn why.

When the museum first opened, a number of people were recruited from the New-York Historical Society. This high-caliber group of curators, educators, and administrators worked hard to launch the museum. And the first exhibition, *NYC Sex: How New York Transformed Sex in America,* opened with a statement: We are real. We are legit. This is a museum.

MoSex presented a united front to the outside world. Inside, however, the organization was rife with unrest. The turmoil stemmed partly from the fact that, whereas most museums are run by a seasoned board of directors and many exhaustive layers of hierarchy, it was a single person—Dan Gluck—who had undertaken the enormous task of creating and sustaining the museum. Museum people are a fastidious species. They do things slowly, with methodical, often painstaking research. Entrepreneurs, like Dan, want everything done as soon as humanly possible . . . if not sooner. That, unfortunately, resulted in a major culture clash.

Most of the staff left the museum after its first few years. Whoever didn't leave was let go. So by the time I started, two years after the museum opened, a large number of the professional staff was gone. All that remained were a few hearty souls who had managed to weather the storm.

→● ●←

Out of all the museums in the world, I have to wonder if the Museum of Sex doesn't have the most unlikely origin story. It began one night when Dan, who had recently sold his successful software company, was out having drinks with friends. When a guy wearing a T-shirt for the Museum of UFOs walked past Dan's group at the bar, they started chatting about what other unlikely topics would make for an entertaining museum. As barroom conversations with friends often go, the chatter ultimately circled back to sex. Gluck, a tech entrepreneur with a background in sculptural arts, fascinated by the work of Camille Paglia, suggested that the perfect addition to the stuffy New York museum world would be an intelligent institution dedicated to sex.

This idle banter soon spread through Dan's network of friends, eventually finding its way to print. In the recently sex-sanitized New York City, where the Times Square S&M shops had given way to the M&M store, even the rumor of a museum of sex was big news. With the press hounding him for comment, Dan denied his intent to establish a museum dedicated to sex. The more he refuted, the more the journalists probed. They were completely convinced his denial was a ploy to throw them off the scent of a good story. But their dogged interest got Dan thinking, and the Wharton grad realized that maybe a museum of sex should be more than hypothetical. And he started to seriously envision a "Smithsonian of Sex."

Odds were not in his favor. The Museum of Sex was dubbed

a "Museum of Smut" by William Donohue of the Catholic League. Dan's project was denied not-for-profit status by the Board of Regents, who stated, "A museum of sex [makes] a mockery of the concept of museums." Still, despite such early and aggressive dismissal, or maybe because of it, Dan carried on with his project and gave himself a crash course in museum directorship.

→◆ ◆←

Ryan sat me down in the conference room.

The only natural light came from three or four small windows that looked straight across the alley into the eccentric Gershwin Hotel, famous for the glass phalli that sprout from its awning. A fitting view.

We started talking, and it became clear that Ryan was just as uncomfortable interviewing me as I was being interviewed. He cleared his throat, and I surveyed the room . . . and hundreds of VHS porn tapes that were piled waist-high along the walls. I'd later learn that these '80s artifacts were a recent acquisition that comprised over nine hundred boxes of erotic content, including silicone molds of famous porn stars' vaginas.

"So I don't have a list of questions. Your résumé looks great. I figured we could just chat. Get to know each other," he suggested. I was happy for the informality, but this was starting to feel more like a blind date than a job interview.

But we soon discovered we had a shared love of surfing. "When you called me I was in the middle of painting my boyfriend's surfboard," I said, excited we had a common passion, but also concerned that this unorthodox interview would not, in fact, lead to a job offer. Shouldn't we be talking about Foucault or museology or something? But Ryan seemed genuinely interested.

Somewhere between describing my favorite surf breaks, telling him about my fieldwork in Venezuela, and recounting the time my host family convinced me to eat a marble-size fish eye (meant to be a great honor), I forgot I was on an interview. An hour passed. Then Ryan walked me to the door.

"Great meeting you, Sarah. I knew you were qualified for the job; I just had to make sure you were MoSex normal. Some of the summer interns I hired were a little questionable in that department."

What was MoSex normal? I would eventually come to realize it meant being not only extremely professional (that is, not using the job to accumulate sexual experiences) but also fully comfortable jumping into a job that involved torpedo tit latex catsuits, ass locks, glory holes, artificial hymens, the secret world of Syrian underwear, nineteenth-century brothel guides, fetish illustrators, scrotal saline injections, sex machines, and panda porn. Yes, panda porn.

"Let me chat with a few people here and I'll get back in touch very soon," Ryan said, shaking my hand. "Just to confirm: You're able to start right away?"

I gave him a yes. A big, happy yes.

three

Vamps and Virgins

On my first day of work, I was presented with a raft of paperwork and nine hundred boxes of porn. The same boxes I spotted during my interview.

It was all part of the Ralph Whittington collection. Ralph, a former librarian at the Library of Congress, had spent some thirty years collecting pornography and cataloging it methodically, in the same manner he did in his professional career. I've always found it endearing that Ralph even had his own "Ralph Whittington Library" stamp, its pressed red ink found on every title page of every single book in the collection.

Ralph would be the first "sex collector" I met in person.

When I bring up the subject of "sex collectors," people often imagine someone from the show *Hoarders* and substitute old newspapers, children's clothes, and cereal boxes for any and all items related to sex. But not all sex collectors have huge collections. And not all sex collectors want attention for it. In fact, I think the majority of sex collectors keep their interest to themselves, which is why these collections are so hard to find. Usually these caches aren't discovered until someone dies. Nevertheless, no matter the size of the collection, these individuals (in my experience, often men) share a devotion to amassing objects associated with sexual pleasure. While some sex collectors, like Ralph, have what we might consider to be "normal" careers, others have made sex the center of their professional identities.

Many sex collectors I've encountered are quite protective of their collections. And for good reason. Admitting that you're a sex collector is very different from acknowledging that you collect, say, stamps. People may be intrigued, but they are just as likely to be judgmental. That's why it's important to gain a collector's trust. Collectors have to know that the museum is going to respect them, their collections, and their sexual identities—something the mainstream world often fails to do.

Ralph's collection was impressive. Each box was marked with neat Sharpie handwriting: ANAL INTRUDER, ANALINGUS, ANNA KOURNIKOVA, AQUATIC SEX, ASS ARTIST, BARBIE DOLL, BETTIE PAGE, BROOKE SHIELDS, BURLESQUE, CARS & GIRLS, CICCIOLINA, CORSETS, DEBBIE DOES DALLAS, EJACULA, ELIZABETH TAYLOR, EROTIC AWARD SHOWS, GOOD VIBRATIONS, HUGE CLITS, etc. (To this day, I dream of making a public installation of just the boxes.) Each contained a handwritten checklist of its contents that could be used to cross-reference and organize the approximately fifteen thousand individual items in his collection.

The boxes housed a broad and robust assortment, objects ranging from 8 mm films, beta and VHS tapes, DVDs, films, and miscellaneous historical ephemera pertaining to each topic. The Whittington Barbie box contains a vintage-inspired "Lingerie Barbie" doll, introduced in 2000, specifically for adult Barbie enthusiasts. The Marilyn Chambers box (star of *Behind the Green Door* and one of the first well-known porn stars of the 1970s) includes a box of Ivory Snow baby detergent, featuring an innocent-looking Chambers snuggling an infant. Chambers, an unknown actress at the time, secured the Ivory Snow gig because she had the girl-next-door looks the company thought best portrayed their image of purity. In fact, the tagline on the box reads: 99 44/100% PURE. When, a year or so into the ad campaign, the spokesperson for purity became one of the country's most well-known porn stars, the company had to sever the connection—and fast. Few of these packages remain in existence, which explains why this perfectly preserved box, although not a typical sex object, is a pop culture sex collector's dream. That's just the tip of the pornographic iceberg.

Ralph was proud to have his collection acquired by the museum, but because he lived in Clinton, Maryland, a MoSex staffer had to go to his house and pick up all the stuff with a truck. What an excursion that was. It took several large U-Haul trucks to transport Ralph's boxes of porn to New York City. And because the universe has a sense of humor, the trucks were randomly stopped by highway patrol for inspection. You can imagine the looks on the officers' faces when the back gates were cranked open to reveal explicitly labeled boxes of porn, blow-up dolls, and racy magazines. Ralph's large collection of functional molds and replicas of porn stars' vaginas and asses were in the trucks, as were photos of Ralph with an assortment of topless adult film stars.

(Chessie Moore and her 36H breasts make several appearances. In 1995, Ralph actually ended up in one of her films, a "dream come true" as he described it on *The Daily Show*.)

Shock factor aside, the part of Ralph's collection that I found most impressive was his library.

Do you want to know about carnival burlesque and traveling sex shows from the 1960s? You've got it here. How about the autobiography of every golden era porn star? Or maybe you'd like to peruse *Cock Sucking for Wives and Mistresses and Sweethearts* as well as *Masturbation with Style* and *Pussy Eating for Everybody*. Yes, there was something for everyone in this particular library.

Ralph was proud of his collection, and very attached to it. Every few months or so he'd check in at the museum. He was a bit of a lingerer; he wanted to reconnect to his life's work and chat. This was great because, over time, he shared his story, which gave me tremendous insight into my new field.

I was expecting a man very different from the one who greeted me in those first weeks of working at the museum. Ralph had deep-blue eyes and a light Southern drawl. He was exceedingly polite and never said anything that felt inappropriate, even though all of our exchanges were about sex. He had been married once and had a daughter a few years older than me. When his grandson was born, someone gave the baby a T-shirt that read, BOOB GUY JUST LIKE GRANDPA.

Ralph lived with his ninety-year-old mother, but that didn't deter him from stacking every room of the house with boxes of porn. By that time, he had established himself as the "king of porn." Ralph and his collection even gained the attention of Jon Stewart's *The Daily Show*. (His mother, too, was featured on *The*

Daily Show, where correspondent Mo Rocca asked her, "Does the sea of porn ever distract you from your crocheting?")

Ralph says he first had the stirrings of a shoe fetish when he was a little boy, sitting in the pews in church, hearing the *click click* of women's high heels as they approached the altar for communion. Although he has his particular fetishes, such as high heels and extraordinarily large breasts, his collection is not specific to his personal preferences. In this way Ralph is different from most collectors, who focus on their own area of interest. Ralph simply collects everything and anything that has to do with sex.

—→◆ ◆←—

There was no real orientation period at MoSex. No on-the-job training. No supervisor to take me through the steps and say, "This is how you do it." It was more of a *listen and learn* environment. Or maybe, *sink or swim.* Thank goodness MoSex had an open-plan office where I was able to hear everything that was going on around me. From my vantage point in my little cubicle it became very clear, very quickly, that putting together an exhibition required an environment similar to staging a theatrical production. Which is to say, all kinds of crazy. You just had to jump right in and do what's needed.

And so I jumped right in to the world of porn.

I first worked on *Vamps and Virgins: The Evolution of the Pin-Up (1860–1960),* curated by Jennifer Kabat. I helped with the installation itself, actually helping to build the exhibition. It was a much more physically demanding job than I realized. I spent a lot of time running errands, finding this tool or that instrument. I hauled artwork from our third-floor office to the ground-floor gallery and spent a fair amount of time climbing up and down ladders. A lot of ladders.

Like everything at the museum, my work on *Vamps and Virgins* was a learning experience and something of a crash course. The exhibition traced the development of the classic American pinup photo from early hard-core imagery in the mid-nineteenth century to the cheesecake images of the 1950s, making it clear that people have been taking "dirty" photos for a very, very long time. The exhibition was composed of the incredible vintage pornography collection of Mark Rotenberg. Unlike Ralph Whittington, Mark Rotenberg became a collector of vintage erotica by accident.

When Mark's elderly neighbor passed away, his Brooklyn Heights street soon became home to a Dumpster full of erotic images, pinups, and pulpy girlie magazines. When Mark realized that this treasure was headed for the landfill, his collector gene was triggered. By saving this collection and continuing to add to it over the next two and a half decades, Mark Rotenberg has become one of the biggest private collectors of vintage erotica today. His collection of ten thousand images was the focus of the Taschen book *Forbidden Erotica,* positioning Mark as *the* authority on the naughty images of the past century.

The exhibition was a real eye-opener for me.

Every generation thinks it's the first to discover erotic sex or that the sex it has is somehow more cutting edge, more kinky, or more "real" than the generations before. Vintage erotica/pornography proves that our ancestors were just as hard-core as we are—if not more so.

It's hard to do justice to the allure of these vintage photographs, but reviewer "Tamii" captures the appeal of the Mark

Rotenberg collection in his or her comments on Amazon (February 19, 2006):

> From seeing this book, I'm now a lover of antique erotica.
> I've seen some stuff from the past and the quality was
> not good, but the photos in this book are absolutely
> wonderful, sexy, and for the most part in great condition.
> I was definitely surprised by the condition of the
> photographs!

We may have technology that makes it easy to record sex, but that doesn't mean we were the first to do so. Naked photographs have existed as long as photography itself. Nude black-and-white photos were developed in France in the early 1800s and peddled euphemistically as "artist studies." The models tended to be women already on the fringes of society who occupied the worlds of dance, theater, and prostitution—fields considered nearly interchangeable at the time. The women of burlesque and vaudeville were also popular subjects because they were willing to show a little ankle, a little décolletage, and sometimes a whole lot more. "French postcards," printed on pocket-size four-by-six-inch card stock, featuring many of these women in various states of nudity were precursors to the men's magazines and pinup calendars of the twentieth century.

Some of these early images, now centuries old, were not what you'd expect. They weren't sedate, simple nude depictions of the body. They featured group sex, cum shots, sex toys, and elements of fetish. They are just as hard-core as the most hard-core images we produce today, even if the bodies were a little more fleshy and a lot hairier.

Although just as graphic as contemporary porn, key differences exist in how early pornographic images were produced and sold. Typically, images were sold in sets of eight, which were specifically designed to show the progression of a true-to-life sexual encounter, mimicking the anticipation built by a slow striptease. And these pornographic photo series were often intentionally humorous. It's as if the Victorians—despite their reputation—didn't take things too seriously. Somehow, when you look at Victorian porn (whether moving or still), you feel like everyone is in on the joke, that even the performers themselves find it kind of funny to be having sex in front of the camera. Seems as if the Victorians knew how to capitalize on the unnaturalness and awkwardness that make amateur porn one of the largest and most lucrative niches today. So while they may not have known their best angles or how best to show off their blow job skills for the camera, they nevertheless seemed to have fun doing it.

Props and comedic setups were common. The salesman paying a visit to the lonely housewife was a common trope. And oral sex and food jokes seemed to have gone hand in hand, too. I once saw a whole series about a man's penis being confused for a hot dog by his partner.

In the old days, porn had a punch line, not just a money shot.

When *Vamps* came to a close, I was given the task of working with Mark Rotenberg to oversee the return of all the artifacts on loan. After almost a year on the job, this stressful assignment was almost like a final exam. I wasn't actually meant to take on this task, but I was the only person in the office when he came to collect his images, so it was up to me to rise to the occasion and put to good use the skills I had learned over the past year.

With my white cotton curatorial gloves, I sat with Mark and the hundreds of images the museum borrowed for the exhibition; I felt like I was part surgeon and part lady out for tea. When a museum receives items from a collector, it issues a condition report. Think of it as the museum version of the rental car checklist. When you rent a car, you're given a diagram to indicate where the dents and scratches exist. When the car is returned, this process is repeated. If damage is found, it's clear in whose care the damage occurred. Museums go through pretty much the same process. A collection's condition report is like a visual dissection, requiring patience and a slow, steady hand. It is also unbelievably nerve-racking. This was my first extended encounter with a sex collector, and Mark taught me rule number one in dealing with any collector: care and precision.

For hours Mark and I compared notes from the incoming paperwork, making sure the outgoing paperwork was the same. It was painstaking, detail-oriented work. We went through every single image, inspected the edges and corners, looking for wear and tear. Not easy when you consider that some of the items were more than one hundred years old. Or that porn isn't always handled with care by its users. I slowly and carefully picked up each individual photo from the stack of hundreds.

One of the images caught my eye. It looked eerily like my grandmother in her modeling days in the early fifties. I couldn't get the resemblance out of my mind, so one night I called and told her about her doppelganger.

"Sarah, come on," she said. I took her response as neither a denial nor acceptance, but the image stuck in my head for months. Finally, I asked Mark if he knew any details about the model's identity. Not knowing why I was so interested, he just said it was an unknown model taken by an unknown photographer, a typical occurrence in the genre.

Grandma's secret was safe. But to this day . . . I wonder.

→◆ ◆←

Next up: *Stags, Smokers and Blue Movies: The Origins of Pornographic Film in America.* This wonderful exhibition was co-curated by Jennifer Lyon Bell, an Amsterdam-based filmmaker whose focus was making porn for women, and Professor Joseph Slade, who wrote the three-volume *Pornography and Sexual Representation: A Reference Guide.* I guess you could say I learned at the feet of the masters.

The *Stags* exhibition highlighted early-American pornographic films, affectionately known as "stags," "smokers," and "blue movies." These films were the gold standard in porn from shortly after the turn of the twentieth century until the mid-1960s. Although Americans weren't the first to put sex on film, we largely dominated its production since the 1920s.

Originally shown at all-male gatherings, such as elk lodges, fraternity houses, and bachelor parties (aka stag parties, from which the nickname emerged), these pornographic films were viewed at group events. For a lot of the guys, stags were the most explicit sex they had been exposed to. Outside of a mysterious lecture about cleanliness, most Americans received no other form of sex education or sex instruction. Unfortunately, stag films often served as a tool of misinformation, mostly because they looked at sex exclusively from the perspective of a heterosexual male. Little attention was given to how to please a woman sexually. Lesbianism, for example, was constructed as the result of a lack of available men, rather than its own sexual identification. As for gay male relationships, they were shown to be the result of an "accidental" threesome, if at all. What's more, male audiences would boo if shown gay sex, as they couldn't publicly "approve" of watching this content.

Most of the sex in these films was heterosexual vaginal intercourse, broken up with bouts of fellatio. The sex featured in stags in no way represented the full spectrum of sexuality, nor did it typically emphasize techniques to satisfy a woman. Both anal sex or sexual acts between men were rare, and BDSM (bondage, discipline, dominance, submission, sadism, masochism) dynamics didn't emerge until the 1950s.

For about fifty dollars, a group of men could treat themselves to somewhere between five and ten films, most of which "starred" people desperate for cash: prostitutes, out-of-work actors, and sailors. Some tried to conceal their identities with wigs, greasepaint, false noses, and masks; others made no such attempt. Far from professional endeavors, the films were often projected against a wall or a suspended bedsheet. The producers often acted as projectionists in those early days, bringing their wares to eager groups of men. Distribution channels and middlemen didn't emerge until later decades. Often the films were seized and confiscated by corrupt police officials who would turn around and rent out the films themselves, providing local men with an opportunity to "blow off steam."

It's different today. Now porn is most often a singular experience, viewed in private on a television, computer, or smartphone. Back then, when watching a stag was an experience to be shared with thirty or so of your best friends—or even the entire football team—the unspoken rule was to keep it in your pants.

We did a lot of research to prepare for the exhibit; nevertheless, all the information we uncovered failed to tell us what it was really like to attend a stag viewing. So, to add dimension to the exhibition, the curatorial team decided to interview men who had actually been to these screenings. Filmed interviews of these men, along with a short bio, were included in the gallery alongside twenty or so flickering stag films, projected in a dark gallery on large platforms that rose like pornographic stalagmites from the floor. The designers cleverly used this technique to stay true to how the films had originally been projected. In having to look down upon the films, they became "artifacts" of a bygone era and forced patrons to engage with "pornographic" content from a new perspective. The interviews of our stag-viewing gentlemen were placed in little peep booths, turning the expectation of these little alcoves on its head. In our inverted peep booths, these men, now in their late fifties to late seventies, reminisced about what it was like to see these films as teenagers, in some cases as young as fourteen.

For most men, watching these films was as close to a sex talk as they ever got. Each discussed the embarrassment of watching graphic sexual content with a room full of their peers, trying hard to hide their pubescent arousal. There was Michael, born in 1947, who watched his first film with several close friends in the apartment adjacent to a bar owned by a family friend. George, a retired college English teacher, attended only one stag event in 1956. He was twenty-one at the time and in a campus suite with thirty or forty other students, mostly jocks from another fraternity. And then there was Leslie, who saw his first stag at the age of fourteen in a friend's home across the street from where he lived in Queens.

My favorite interview was with a slightly sheepish man in his early sixties who described how he had internalized his observation. No matter the sex act on-screen, this man observed, the men involved in the stag film never removed their black dress socks. As an inexperienced newlywed, he emulated this dress code with his new bride. A few months into their marriage, his puzzled wife had to explain that socks weren't a requirement for the act. Years later I told this story while on a panel discussing the ethics of porn and its impact on sex education, and this wardrobe choice in the movies was finally explained: "For leverage," Sinnamon Love, a performer and director, shared with me and the entertained audience. In that moment, I imagined how pleased my bashful interviewee would be for this clarifying exchange.

I was impressionable in those early days. Although I knew the theory behind gender politics, hierarchical structures, and all of that academic jargon that makes people's eyes glaze over, I was in no way prepared for the realities of the Museum of Sex: the nitty-gritty of what people are thinking, doing, creating, and fantasizing about on a minute-by-minute basis. All the theory in the world couldn't prepare me for sex machines, invitations to sex clubs, or visits to dungeons. Thank goodness for Professor Slade, who not only filled my head with film titles such as *Johnny Twat Sucker* and *George and the Blonde* but also imparted the invaluable wisdom I would use throughout my MoSex tenure: every technology is eventually used for sex. The combination of Slade's and Bell's perspectives—one highly academic and one from the world of porn production—was critical in my erotic education. While working on the exhibition, I learned a great deal from both, not just about porn and its history, but also about the relationship between technology (in this case, film) and sex.

→◆ ◆←

Working as a researcher on *Stags, Smokers and Blue Movies* was an education, and I was eager to dive into curating—not just researching the subject, but choosing what would actually compose the exhibition. I was in awe of the process and thrilled to be learning on the job. As a graduate student I was obsessed with absorbing information, and working on *Stags* showed me how I could turn that knowledge into a product that people actually want to consume, something that could reach far beyond the influence of the ivory tower. I needed to be patient, though, because during those first projects, I was really working on the sidelines. Who could have predicted my first job would be an apprenticeship in sex?

four

The Heinous Sin of Self-Pollution

John Vollmer is the gentleman curator of your imagination. Gray hair and glasses, eloquent and erudite, he's knowledgeable, worldly, and refined. All that's missing is the pocket watch. John comes across as the type of man who can speak authoritatively on any topic, whether it's where to find the best restaurant in Paris or the best tailor in Milan. And he's the real thing: a distinguished scholar and independent curator who directs projects and creates individual exhibits for universities, museums, and private collections. How lucky for me that he'd end up playing an instrumental role in my life at MoSex. (And, in the world of coincidence, it was John who had actually curated *Sex Among the Lotus,* the exhibition that had prompted me to inquire about working at MoSex.)

Our first project together was the museum's *Spotlight on the Permanent Collection Gallery,* conceptualized as a funhouse for the academically and sexually curious. I assisted John in assembling the exhibition from the nearly fifteen thousand artifacts belonging to the Museum of Sex, as well as items on long-term loan. It was a massive project.

John and I organized the exhibition around both theme and time period, filling the gallery with a miscellany of items ranging from the controversial (photos from a 1938 *Life Magazine* of a woman giving birth—the visibility of labia caused people to cancel their subscriptions) to those at the heart of legal battles (Henry Miller's novel *Tropic of Cancer,* which was banned for its sexually candid content) to original costumes, photos, and signs from New York's Harmony Burlesque. Basically, our aim was to showcase centuries of material created with the simple goal of titillation and to invite our patrons to explore sexuality in a way that's "personal and pertinent" to their own desires and experiences.

At the entrance to the exhibition we stationed a wooden "cabinet of curiosities," a nod to the original format of museums, displaying antique gynecological tools, vintage corsets, and a copy of the infamous *Memoirs of a Woman of Pleasure,* otherwise known as *Fanny Hill* (an eighteenth-century *Fifty Shades of Grey*). Published in 1749, *Fanny Hill* is the story of a young, naive country orphan who moves to London and becomes a prostitute and a mistress. Within the first few pages, Fanny, a fourteen-year-old virgin, engages in lesbian sex with a prostitute. The book was banned on both sides of the Atlantic. As the focus of America's first obscenity case in 1821, Fanny Hill can claim the title of being patient zero in America's obsession with the obscene.

The novel offers descriptions of the first erection Fanny witnessed, "her sturdy stallion had now unbuttoned, and produced naked, stiff and erect, that wonderful machine," and the first acts of intercourse she observed: "He gently pushed her down. . . . Her thighs were spread out to their utmost extension, and discovered between them the mark of the sex, the red-centered cleft of flesh, whose lips vermillioning inwards, expressed a small ruby line." The author, John Cleland, didn't hesitate to provide graphic descriptions of the vagina. He also didn't hold back in describing seminal fluid, seduction, group sex, and male homosexual sex, which was not only taboo at the time but also illegal and highly punishable.

Good thing for Cleland he was already in debtors' prison when he wrote the novel.

The bulk of erotic literature was not accessible to the average person; sex on the page was kept under wraps. Literally. It was published in limited editions, privately distributed, and sold at prohibitively high prices. In 1882, an erotic novel would cost the average laborer nearly two weeks' salary.

A library was a status symbol in the nineteenth century. Books were rare and special objects, so having a collection of them—a library, that is—really meant something. Erotic books (especially those with erotic illustrations) were even more rare. Bawdy stories were shared in public houses, of course, but only the wealthy could actually afford to possess erotic literary artifacts. And because the wealthy felt it was their duty to protect common people from these objects (commoners were without education and could be easily corrupted—or so the argument went), these erotic libraries existed under the protection of wealthy men.

Many elite libraries were filled with sexually graphic poems and prose. Explicit depictions of the juicier scenes from *Fanny Hill* and its copycats were even sold as engravings for those who wanted a bit of visual stimulation with their literary erotica. These libraries long managed to fly under the radar of the ever-shifting category of obscenity, at least until the mid-1800s.

Proud of their "pornography" (a term not used until 1858), some early collectors created erotic ex libris, or bookplates, to declare their ownership of a book. These marques often featured imagery of nudes, sexual intercourse, and bestiality. Because they usually contained an inscription such as "from the library of . . . ," these ex libris were important in providing provenance to a book.

Whereas some collectors feared discovery, and in some cases even burned their own books, others believed they were beyond reproach. Such was the case of Lord Spencer Ashbee, who forced the British Museum to take his huge collection of erotica in exchange for donating his highly coveted Cervantes collection. Contradictory attitudes and reactions to erotica have deep historical roots, and many of the battles regarding obscenity rest in this divide. In some ways the historical controversy over obscenity has set up the modern dichotomy between the erotic art sold in galleries and pornography sold through inexpensive, populist channels. If it's expensive, it's art. It it's not expensive, it's porn. The Museum of Sex aims to disrupt this very distinction by showing both the "high" and "low" of sex, often side by side.

That's what our *Spotlight Gallery* was all about. In addition to antique erotica like *Fanny Hill* and the graphic engravings that accompanied it, we rounded out the exhibition with pinup photographs, sex education videos from the 1950s, vintage condoms packaged in tiny tin cases, holograms made out of NASA-grade technology, burlesque costumes, peep show tokens, sex dolls, sex machines, and antique vibrators.

We also filled the walls with fine art, including a 1968 etching by Pablo Picasso called *Raphael and the Fornarina XI: The Pope Is Open-Mouthed in His Armchair.* This bawdy sketch, which satirizes the pope watching a couple engaged in a sexual act, was inspired by Jean-Auguste-Dominique Ingres's drawing *Raphael et la for-narina* (1814), which itself was inspired by Raphael's *La fornarina*, painted some three hundred years earlier in 1518. (The in-joke here is that Raphael, a Vatican favorite, was rumored to have died while having sex with his mistress Margherita Luti, the woman thought to have posed as "la fornarina.") Next to the raunchy Picasso were hung works by artist and activist Keith Haring, who became famous for a particular graffiti/street-art style honed in public art installations and New York City subway stations during the early 1980s, as well as for being one of the many artists who was lost to the HIV/AIDS pandemic. Haring's bold prints (criticized by some for their cartoonish quality, praised by others for their intensity) worked well next to the Picasso. Though Haring's work features seemingly simplistic block figures engaged in graphic homosexual orgies and Picasso's sketch harkens back to the sixteenth century, both serve as important reminders that more than a few greats have been known to make erotic art.

Nevertheless, not all venues are able to exhibit such explicit works. Federal funding and taxpayer dollars can make exhibiting "erotic art" not just problematic but impossible for many cultural institutions. Maybe this is why Peter Norton and the Lannon family, prominent figures at more traditional museums, donated sizable collections of erotic fine art to the Museum of Sex. Perhaps it was exciting to know these works might find a home that would properly showcase rather than simply relegate them to the depths of storage.

→◆ ◆←

Working on the *Spotlight Gallery* with John Vollmer was a privilege. John had an air of sophistication and diplomacy that was so important for the museum in those early days. He knew how to have the right conversations and how to "speak museum"—qualities that were critical for the organization's growth. John loved the work he did, and his knowledge seemed unlimited. I was in awe of him.

Through John's mentoring, I began to understand how in-the-flesh encounters can really engage visitors and help bring about a greater understanding of the world of sex. And because MoSex is able to display artifacts that might otherwise be hidden from public view, we really can expand our patrons' horizons and help to dispel misconceptions. But it's got to be memorable. Which is why, I guess, John taught me about creating the "sticky moment."

Every exhibition should be filled with a few sticky moments, displays so engaging, shocking, beautiful, or inciting that they force a patron to stop, read, and absorb. Which brings me to the highlight of the exhibition, a nineteenth-century anti-onanism device. Basically, a contraption to deter masturbation.

The anti-onanism device, which was made in France in the late 1800s, was displayed in its own under-lit case in the exhibit. It was composed of a thick, slightly perforated brown leather harness molded in the shape of a wide weightlifter's belt. Attached was the sinister addition of a steel perforated cup that encased the wearer's scrotum, along with a constricting metal sheath where the penis was inserted. Besides a small hole for the passage of urine, the downward curved sheath covered the entirety of the penis, not only preventing penile manipulation but also making an erection painful, if not impossible, for the boys and young men forced to wear them.

About the size of a medium pair of Underoos, this contraption was most likely worn by a prepubescent boy of eight or nine. Two metal straps cinched the harness tight around the hips and the ring below the scrotal cage was secured to a strap pulled between the user's legs, locking it into place. The device's creators ensured this contraption wasn't going anywhere. Almost anyone with a penis involuntarily shudders when viewing this artifact.

The term "anti-onanism" points to the Bible and a man named Onan who was punished for "spilling his seed." Onanism, auto-eroticism, and masturbation were historically interchangeable words for the act of self-pleasuring, which was thought to cause madness, lethargy, physical deformities, and mental retardation. These ideas were given legitimacy in the pages of *Onania; or, The Heinous Sin of Self-Pollution, and All Its Frightful Consequences,* a work published in 1723. Worse, they were brought to life by horrendous illustrations of bulbous-eyed, hairy-palmed, bug-eyed "self-abusers" who quite effectively communicated the author's concerns.

Onania's authors positioned masturbation as a serious public enemy, and by invoking the obscure biblical reference, they hoped to establish their credibility. Credibility was key if they were to convince the public of masturbation's disastrous effects and successfully sell their miracle device that could remedy this abominable and, let's be honest, ubiquitous act. The antimasturbation business proved an entrepreneurial gold mine: everyone needed a cure. This negative attitude toward masturbation originated from a harsh but successful eighteenth-century medical scam that perpetuated a shameful attitude toward sexuality and lasted for centuries.

The popularity of *Onania* spread throughout Europe and the United States, inspiring a large tradition of tonics and devices. Hundreds and hundreds of patents have been filled with the U.S. patent office for preventing and controlling masturbation, including a penis fan, designed to stave off heat to the genitals, a testicle Taser, and a "warning system," in which a bell would ring if a boy experienced an erection. As late as the mid-1970s, patents were still being filed for instruments and implements to get people's hands out of their pants.

And it wasn't just devices. A bland diet was also believed to cure young men of masturbatory tendencies. Americans J. H. Kellogg and Sylvester Graham, best known for inventing corn flakes and graham crackers, originally produced their famous products as masturbatory remedies. Sincere believers in the dire consequences of self-pleasure, Kellogg and Graham purposefully marketed bland foods crafted to quell dangerous internal passions. As Kellogg so confidently states in his publication, "Plain Facts for Young and Old":

> Exciting stimulants and condiments weaken and irritate his nerves and derange the circulation. Thus, indirectly, they affect the sexual system, which suffers through sympathy with the other organs. But a more direct injury is done. Flesh, condiments, eggs, tea, coffee, chocolate, and all stimulants, have a powerful influence directly upon the reproductive organs. They increase the local supply of blood; and through nervous sympathy with the brain, the passions are aroused.

Nervous sympathy with the brain, indeed.

five

A Sex Education

Despite Ryan's assessment that I was well qualified for the job at the museum, the truth was, I knew very little about the history of sex. I hadn't heard the rumors of Cleopatra's bee-powered vibrator, nor did I know that the celibate Gandhi slept next to nude women to test his resolve. I wasn't familiar with Annie Sprinkle, whose performance piece *A Public Cervix Announcement* in 1992 invited hundreds of art goers to look inside her cervix, aided by a speculum and flashlight. And I certainly didn't know that an abundance of vaginal applicators found in archaeological sites indicates that the domicile was once a brothel. (These syringes were used to maintain health, treat venereal disease, and prevent pregnancy.) But I was industrious as well as ambitious, so I worked hard—sometimes a little too hard—to absorb information through long hours of cramming. Basically, I spent most of 2004 (and the next decade) with my nose jammed in some kind of sex book.

Fortunately, I had access to a very special, one-of-a-kind resource: the library at MoSex. A literary sanctuary where books will never be banned or locked away, the library at MoSex, with its unique stockpile of books, is open to researchers on a case-by-case basis. For me, it's been a refuge and a location of revelation—my own personal reference library. I've raided its shelves, Post-it-noting its pages for nearly a decade.

The library at MoSex is a treasure trove for sex bibliophiles. Some books have been donated, some purchased as research for specific exhibitions, and others sent along by eager publishers trying to get their work into the museum's shop. And some books have a more prestigious past. When *Playboy*'s library officially closed a few years back, the Museum of Sex saved thousands of books. The Playboy collection functioned on a true library system, complete with check-out cards with the handwritten names of borrowers—making these sleeves and slips artifacts in their own right.

Over the years several collectors, some eager to be known and others preferring to remain anonymous, have also helped add to the diversity of our collection.

I had these amazing resources at my fingertips and I took full advantage. I read about sex everywhere: at work, at the odd cafe in Greenwich Village, in between classes, and on the subway. One of my creative colleagues even created nondescript brown paper book covers so I wouldn't get unwelcome attention while reading *The Art of Vaginal Fisting* or *The Multi Orgasmic Man* during NYC rush hour. As a graduate student expected to read a thousand pages a week, I was primed for this kind of intensive study. Still, there were times when I really wished there was a CliffsNotes guide for sex curating.

One of the more fascinating areas of my research was on the sex experiments that took place in the early to mid-twentieth century—and still continue today—in the name of furthering science. For instance, I was totally enthralled with a device that measured orgasms when inserted in the vagina. This coloscope, appropriately nicknamed Ulysses, was a long cylindrical mechanism attached to a small camera. The coloscope's mastermind? William Masters, of Masters and Johnson fame.

William Masters and Virginia Johnson were an unlikely team. When they began working together in 1957, Masters was a prominent St. Louis gynecologist, and Johnson—a former singer totally uncredentialed in the medical field—was his secretary. Although Johnson lacked a formal scientific background, her bedside manner was critical in convincing subjects to participate in their unorthodox research: sex in the lab. Subjects had to agree to being hooked up to monitors and engage in intercourse (or be sexually stimulated) while scientists observed and took notes. Without Johnson, the project wouldn't have been possible.

Masters and Johnson had an intense personal relationship that was volatile and notorious. It went from professional to sexual to married and eventually divorced, over the course of nearly five decades. Nevertheless, together they were able to gather sexual data that had, up to that point, only been the subject of rumor and hearsay. They identified four phases of human sexual arousal: the excitement phase, the plateau phase, the orgasmic phase, and the resolution phase. Their research included observing over ten thousand "complete cycles" of the four-pronged sexual response, and their data established a long-standing model for the arc of human sexual response.

One of the interesting nuances of their findings was that although each of the initial stages was based on an intensification of the body's reaction to stimulation, data showed that not all sexual experiences necessarily resulted in the orgasmic phase for both or either participant: women lacked a refractory period, the time after orgasm when men are typically unable to ejaculate. Therefore, the ability to achieve multiple orgasms was predominantly female. In the eyes of Masters and Johnson, women were the true sexual athletes of our species—a startling medical assertion for the late 1950s.

Without Masters and Johnson, we would probably still think having sex during pregnancy is dangerous (no, your penis is not going to hit the baby in the head), or that sex has to stop at a certain age (the skyrocketing rates of sexually transmitted diseases at retirement homes proves that notion a fallacy). Their research, which continued until the 1990s, dispelled many widely held misconceptions about sexuality.

Not only was I unfamiliar with Masters and Johnson before coming to the Museum of Sex, I didn't even know about Alfred Kinsey, the man considered to be the founder of American sex research and whose work set the stage for researchers like Masters and Johnson.

Like me, Kinsey never set out to study sex. Dr. Kinsey was a Harvard-trained zoologist who worked as an entomologist at Indiana University. But it was his lack of sexual knowledge that led to a seismic shift in his career—from organisms to orgasms. Kinsey was in his midtwenties when he met Clara McMillan at a university department function. After a chaste courtship, they married the following year. But the couple had practically no sexual experience or knowledge prior to their relationship, and it took them almost a year to consummate the marriage. We can only speculate what went on in the Kinsey bedroom. Clara and Dr. Kinsey may even have consulted one of the many "marriage manuals" in circulation at the time. But these books and pamphlets usually advocated self-control and were devoid of any useful information. This gave Kinsey an idea. In 1938, alongside a petition from Indiana University's Association of Women Students, Kinsey began teaching a scientific birds-and-bees course for students who were married or contemplating marriage.

Kinsey believed that a healthy sexual relationship was vital to a successful marriage and that education and information are vital to a healthy sexual relationship. Unfortunately, while sexuality was being discussed by European sexologists from a psychological perspective (à la Freud and his followers), few were gathering hard data on the physicality of the subject. Limited research was available, but Kinsey considered the information, often based on tiny sample groups, to be largely biased. And he was inspired to change all that.

So Kinsey set out to research human sexuality with one goal in mind: discovering "what people are really doing behind closed doors." Kinsey and his associates gathered over eighteen thousand interviews and oral histories. And what he found was shocking.

Based on his large sample pool, Kinsey determined that Americans were not only having sex younger, more frequently, and in a wider array of positions than expected, they were also engaging with great frequency in acts previously considered rare, such as oral sex.

Kinsey's data on homosexual activity was viewed as particularly scandalous. While he said it was impossible to determine the exact number of people who are either homosexual or heterosexual, his data revealed that 37 percent of men and 13 percent of women had had at least one same-sex experience, and 46 percent of his respondents reported having bisexual attractions. Kinsey even broke down the data based on the kinds of sexual acts performed. For instance, 30 percent of men received fellatio from another man, while only 14 percent had performed fellatio on another man—all astounding statistics for the time period, when same-sex activities were not only closeted but also rendered illegal by various indecency and sodomy laws. (Even disturbing-the-peace laws were used to arrest people suspected of homosexual acts.)

The fluidity of homosexual acts and attractions led Kinsey to establish the Homosexual-Heterosexual Rating Scale, known as the Kinsey Scale. The Kinsey Scale put individuals on a sexual continuum with grades from 0 to 6. Those with no homosexual experience were given a 0, whereas those who were exclusively homosexual earned a 6. Although not a formally administered test, the Kinsey Scale was an exercise in self-evaluation. Based on the extensive data accumulated, Kinsey and his associates realized sexual orientation didn't fit neatly into one box. Like all of his data, correlations were further established based on marital status, age, education, occupation, religious affiliation, geographic origin, rural or urban background, and age at onset of puberty.

But Kinsey's conclusions did not solely rest on interviews and data. Because he spent hours upon end with his interviewees (in some cases partaking in his own erotic explorations), he became a friend and trusted confidant. Kinsey's subjects shared their private journals, artwork, erotic literature and photographs, homemade pornography, and even their private sex collections. Inspired by Kinsey, one collector (Sam Steward—later a focus of an entire MoSex exhibition) created a "Stud File," a card catalog with 746 entries that documented his wealth of sexual partners, acts performed, and the details of his partner's penises. In some cases, he even attached a swatch of the lover's pubic hair to the back of the card.

Through his relationships with Steward and other research participants, Kinsey also began to collect the ephemera of their sexuality. These items ranged from graphic photographs to films of sexual acts, and they even included drawings and personal correspondence. Many of these possessions were considered both obscene and illegal, and they were routinely confiscated by the police. For instance, sending a nude image with visible pubic hair through the mail could lead to jail time. Kinsey's desire to have a confidential repository for his sex research and a vault for his growing sex collection led to the establishment of the Institute for Sex Research in 1947.

Kinsey sold his wealth of research and holdings for one dollar to the institute, whose purpose was (according to the Kinsey Institute's Web site) to "continue research on human sexual behavior; to accept, hold, use, and administer research materials, a library, case histories, and other materials relating to the project." With the help of a cryptographer, a secret organizational system was created to protect the collection and the participants' privacy—a necessary precaution, given that this kind of explicit ephemera could destroy lives. Jail, ostracism, and violent hate crimes were serious realities. For this reason, only Kinsey and his closest research confidants knew the key to the institute's secret codes.

The Institute for Sex Research, now known as the Kinsey Institute for Research in Sex, Gender, and Reproduction, has survived the test of time. The institute has grown to be one of the largest and most comprehensive sex holdings in the world.

→◆ ◆←

John Vollmer and I weren't Masters and Johnson, but he was an invaluable mentor in my curatorial education. John showed me the importance of infinite curiosity and diligent research. He prompted me to question everything. It's amazing how well the book report questions from my childhood helped uncover the truths about sex artifacts. Why was an object made? Who made it? Where did they make it? What is it made out of? Who bought, sold, or donated it? Or the most interesting question of all: How had these often discarded objects come to survive decades, even centuries, of censorship?

A few years back I got a call from a landlord on the Upper West Side of Manhattan describing a tenant who had passed away with no family to claim his belongings. In a thick accent, the landlord made it very clear that the "pile of porn" was going to end up in the Dumpster at the end of the week if we didn't come to review it. The landlord made clear his disapproval for the subject matter—and also his own homophobia.

A pile of porn. And just a subway ride away.

We arrived at a nicely appointed brownstone, where we were met by the gruff landlord. He opened the door to a small studio with furniture thrown into a growing mountain in the middle of the room. Framed art, books, and magazines were carelessly thrown into the mix, with no thought given to these items that once held great value to the owner. As we crossed the threshold, the landlord pointed us to the "pile of porn," a humble stack of tattered magazine clippings and maybe fifty VHS porn tapes, his very reason for summoning us to the apartment. I had incorrectly assumed we would encounter boxes and boxes of items (mass consumption was the typical MO of a large-scale collector). I was a little disappointed.

The recently deceased, it appeared, had for many years ripped out images from gay porn magazines, probably those he found sexually compelling. Although an interesting look into one man's sexuality, this two-foot stack of actively handled pages from magazines and commercially available films was not the treasure I had hoped for.

But as we looked a little closer, the deceased occupant came to life—and so did his collection.

It soon became apparent that our anonymous collector had a great love affair with books, and over the years he had amassed thousands of volumes on topics ranging from art history to travel. But his primary interest seemed to be gay history and politics, a movement he had likely seen take life in New York. Hundreds of rare books, many now out of print, filled floor-to-ceiling bookcases along every wall.

We climbed over the discarded furniture, caked in dust, to get a closer look at this incredible library.

"Forget about those!" the landlord shouted as we made our way up the rickety library-style ladder. "The porn is over there." He pointed in the opposite corner.

"We might be more interested in these," I said, barely turning away from the books, so excited to see such a large and well-preserved collection. He shrugged, waved us off, and returned to dragging boxes out to the Dumpster.

"We have to save these," I said quietly as I handed a few examples to Lizzie.

We only had a few hours before the apartment needed to be completely cleared. Climbing up and down the ladder and on the tops of tables covered with discarded contents, we methodically placed the books into boxes. Our excitement grew along with our pile, and the landlord became visibly worried that he was missing out on a financial opportunity. When he asked us how much we wanted to pay, we simply reminded him that he had already asked us to take away "all the disgusting gay stuff."

A victory in the battle of sexual preservation.

Then there was the time a Brooklyn man contacted the museum when pornographic photos literally came falling out of the woodwork. Hidden in his brownstone a century earlier (to avoid either vice raids or the disapproval of his family), this erotic trove had been liberated by a renovation. A sex curator has to think like a treasure hunter: the thing I seek will not be displayed on mantels; more likely it will be furtively squirreled away, left to accidental discovery.

One such treasure hunt led me to San Francisco—my first business trip. I was tasked with sorting through one of the largest collections of nude, male pornography in existence, a collection created by a man named Bob Mizer.

In the early 1940s, Mizer became captivated by the bodybuilding displays on Venice Beach, California, where scantily clad men oiled up and exhibited their physiques. In 1945, he established a roughly produced pamphlet called "Physique Pictorial" that featured male photographs with explanations of the particular exercises being performed. Sold under the guise of exercise instruction, these periodicals gave gay men access to images of the male body without betraying their orientation. Mizer's photographs captured beautifully toned men, icons of idealized masculinity, wearing nothing more than a posing pouch—a kind of glorified G-string/jock strap combination. According to the Bob Mizer Foundation, Mizer "photographed thousands of men, ranging from Hollywood actors and body-builders to hustlers and porn stars. His portfolio, estimated at nearly one million different images and thousands of films and video tapes, contains photographs of unique cultural figures, including action star and politician Arnold Schwarzenegger, Andy Warhol muse Joe Dallesandro, and contemporary artist Jack Pierson."

But Mizer suffered for his dedication. His house was raided and his pictures were destroyed by the police on several occasions, often on the grounds that pubic hair was visible. Some photographers tried to outsmart the police by covering the genital region of the photograph with a substance that could later be removed by the owner, much like a lottery scratch-off ticket. But this was risky business as police were always on the lookout for homosexual content. Mizer's collection, spanning almost fifty years of photographic obsession, gives testament to a talented photographer and also provides valuable insight into what it meant to be gay during such a hostile era.

Shortly after Bob's death, his collection was scattered. Some items were discarded, some were gifted to people, and other valuables were lost (a tragic and all-too-common end to many collections). Although some works were salvaged by Mizer's friend John Sonsini, somewhere between sixteen and thirty-three Dumpsters were filled with Mizer's archive of sets, props, costumes, and equipment. The rest of the estate was shuffled around before ultimately falling into the able hands of a man named Dennis Bell, who set out to unify the once great collection.

I felt like a detective when I arrived at Dennis's house that first morning. From the outside, the house looked like any other in the quiet suburban block, filled with midcentury bungalows and single-floor ranch houses, nestled among mature trees. My surroundings were comforting, but I was still nervous as to what I might find once Dennis opened the door. I knew it was a great privilege to go through this collection, one I intended to handle with professionalism and respect, but let's face it: going to a stranger's home to sort through sexual items? Well, it is kind of intimidating. But all anxiety dissolved when a warm and welcoming Dennis greeted me that first day. He had only recently acquired the collection and was still trying to figure out the value of the photos and what to do with them. I got a sense that he was happy to have my company—and my perspective.

Dennis ushered me into a room with floor-to-ceiling shelves containing shoe boxes holding 8 mm films, slides, and photographs with old white-edged borders. I sat there for ten hours a day going through it all. Narrowing down the thousands of images to a hundred to take back to the museum was an enormous task. But if I did my job well, it would be easier to whittle that group down to the twenty or thirty pictures needed for the exhibition.

My decisions were based on numerous criteria. From an artistic perspective, I looked at the composition of the photos, noting the way in which Mizer constructed his images, and the way he employed various DIY lighting tricks (using some of his mother's etched crystal bowls to project patterns in the backgrounds, for example). Hoping to construct a narrative about his work, I looked for images that would tell the larger story of his career. For instance, I knew that possessing these kinds of images in the '50s and '60s was a crime and that Bob Mizer had been arrested. So when I came across several images where the penis was cut out, I could infer that this was Mizer's way of skirting the law—an artist torn. Curatorially, I wanted to show how Mizer engaged in his artistic pursuits in the context of such a hostile environment.

But I also wanted to mix it up—show pieces that are a little shocking, then maybe something that's funny, particularly since the collection featured an overwhelming spectrum of both. A curator is always looking to showcase the diversity of a body of work, and at Dennis's house I watched hours and hours of footage featuring naked men wrestling, culminating in the masturbation and penis-measuring scenes that were a hallmark of Mizer's work in the '80s and early '90s. In three days, I saw more penises than I ever thought possible.

six

Men Without Suits

The San Francisco trip, along with John Vollmer's mentorship, rounded out my understanding of the work that goes into exhibitions. With John's encouragement, I was coming to see exhibitions as a work of art in their own right—something to be experienced and valued, something to provoke. Once I understood that the aim of displaying artifacts is to help us expand our horizons—to see ourselves and the world a little differently—and that the aim of our exhibits is to impart knowledge that may shape our understanding of the world, well . . . let's just say my suitcase filled with photos of naked men took on a whole new significance.

John encouraged my ambition to make beautiful and lively exhibitions that seduce people into learning, the same way I had been seduced into this specialized field. And he showed me how the invisible art of the curator creates the thread that ties everything together. Any thought that this was a temporary part-time job, an experiment, or curiosity was long gone. I was serious about my job. What I didn't realize was how serious the job was about me.

In the summer of 2006, two years after I began working at the Museum of Sex, with the ink still fresh on my master's, I was thinking seriously about next steps. In addition to my job as assistant curator at MoSex, I'd taken an internship at El Museo del Barrio, New York City's leading Latino museum dedicated to Puerto Rican, Caribbean, and Latin American art.

I was at a crossroads.

Although I knew how things worked at MoSex, that didn't mean it would work the same way at El Museo del Barrio. Maybe "legit" museums really did work differently. I needed to see if I was cut out for the larger museum world or if this whole unexpected adventure at MoSex had been a fluke. I needed to see if the air really was different up on Museum Mile.

Helping the curatorial team prep for the installation of the traveling exhibition *The Disappeared* was an emotionally intense experience, and exactly the kind of work I had always set out to do. The exhibition brought attention to the plight of the men and women who vanished throughout Latin America at the hands of totalitarian regimes. The fifteen artists in the show hailed from countries that, in the late twentieth century, were ruled by regimes that practiced the stealth removal of political opponents, or who forced these people—*los desaparecidos*—into hiding, often through the apparatus of government-sanctioned murder. Such significant work, and I was proud to be associated with it.

But as the El Museo team hustled through a lot of the same madness of exhibition installation and opening-party celebrations, I realized how much I missed the punk rock attitude of the

Museum of Sex—and how much I had learned working there. More than that, in addition to appreciating the tremendous on-the-job experience I had at MoSex, I also came to understand that the curator's toolbox is much the same, regardless of the institution.

I thought my time at El Museo del Barrio would round out my résumé, and my experience. Then I was offered a job. The stakes were raised.

I talked to John. While not the museum's official curator, he was in many ways the institution's godfather, cultivating a curatorial perspective and helping to shape institutional objectives and vision. He was also my mentor.

"What if you were offered a curator position here?"

I looked at him. "Curator? Are you serious?"

"Yes."

"Obviously I would consider it."

"Consider it? Or strongly consider it?"

I thought about it. El Museo del Barrio was, in some ways, a more "legitimate," more prestigious institution than MoSex. Nevertheless, at a place like that, the chance to be curator would be many, many years away. If ever. But it wasn't just opportunity that pulled me back to MoSex; it was a genuine belief in what the institution could evolve into. I saw it as a ground-floor opportunity to truly make something beyond most people's wildest imaginations.

"Seriously consider it," I replied.

And that, as they say, was that.

→◆ ◆←

I was never bored at the Museum of Sex, never less than inspired. But some installations totally captured my imagination and altered the way I view history. *Mapping Sex in America,* for example. This online, interactive platform encouraged people to plot the locations of their sexual encounters on a map of the United States. Not surprisingly, the data proved that every location can be—and probably has been—used for sex. Artist Steve Lambert captured this sentiment in his collection of typographic prints that read: "We have had sex in this room." "We have had sex in this room also." "Yup, this one too." Although meant to create a point of interaction with anyone who walked into the owner's home and chose to purchase these specific works, these prints addressed a larger and perhaps more unsettling idea: it's likely that someone has, at some time, had sex exactly where you now sit.

The *Mapping Sex in America* project confirmed the unacknowledged truth that sex is the ever-present specter in our physical environments.

One of the highlights of the exhibition was the touch-screen monitor and keyboard we installed to encourage visitors to enter their own sex stories. Those who couldn't get to the museum could log on to our Web site to enter the information of their trysts. Stories arrived with an incredible variety of tone and content. Some were sweet and romantic, whereas others were so clichéd it was difficult to believe they were real. I lost track of the number of accounts that mimicked the plot of cheap porn movies, with some random woman (gorgeous, of course) wandering into a guy's apartment or a stranger pulling someone into a public bathroom. And the orgies! Even with the benefits of Viagra, if I were to believe every entry, I'd think the men and women of this country had superhuman sexual stamina.

Cheeky users often indicated the museum as their own sexual landmarks—more fantasy than reality, I'm guessing. (Unless you count the journalist Bill Schulz, who turned his experience "camping" in our 2015 *Splendor in the Grass: Kinesthetic Camping Ground* exhibition into a sexual opportunity.) Unedited save full names and identifiable details such as phone numbers, the objective behind the project was to archive sex in the twenty-first century, much in the way Alfred Kinsey had decades before. I envisioned the installation as a sexualized version of StoryCorps.

While places like brothels, peep shows, sex clubs, and red-light districts are obvious hot spots of sexual activity, more commonplace locations are also popular choices for sexual trysts. But, of course, bars, hotels, inns, and that unassuming local bed and breakfast all saw their fair share of the action. Not only did nineteenth-century NYC hotels require you, at times, to sleep in the same bed with a stranger, but many bars would add beds to their attics to get around laws that tried to curb consumption, which, not surprisingly, only made prostitution easier. It's incredible how the "right moment" can be created with a little alcohol and a conveniently located bed.

The *Mapping of Sex* installation was closely related to one of my favorite artifacts in the museum's permanent collection: the 1855 and 1856 Brothel Guides. These pocket-size guides had once been a discreet resource for men arriving in New York, eager to fulfill their sexual fantasies.

They say a picture is worth a thousand words, but when it came to this guidebook, the words spoke more to me than a lot of the flesh on display at the museum.

The Guide to the Harem; or, Directory to the Ladies of Fashion in New York and Various Other Cities provided the addresses of brothels and the names of the madams who ran them—sort of a Lonely

Planet guide for nineteenth-century sex. The booklets provided revealing descriptions of the women, accommodations, and services on offer. Most of these locations were downtown in the Soho area—today a trendy neighborhood with socialite residents.

Miss Emma Clifton's house at 29 Mercer Street was described as a "fashionable retreat for the admirers of woman's charms, is fitted up in a most costly manner. The hostess is an accomplished lady, and understands the business to which she has devoted herself. Here, also, may be seen a perfect galaxy of female beauty."

Miss Kate Hastings's "beautiful palace" at 119 Mercer also received high marks. Portrayed as having "obtained great popularity caused by her cow hiding the notorious Ned Buntline" during "a very eccentric trip she made to California," Miss Hastings made quite a name for herself in New York's saturated sex market when she hosted Ned Buntline. Buntline, whose real name was E. Z. C. Judson, was a notorious womanizer who claimed to have discovered Buffalo Bill. Not only had this "King of the Dime Novel" been married seven times, but he had also killed one of his lover's husbands and was one of the biggest names of the day. Such celebrity notoriety—similar to having a notorious A-lister visit your brothel, but much worse—and the implication that "unusual" sex acts were on tap at 119 Mercer, made Miss Hastings and her ladies a big draw.

Although not publicized at Miss Hastings's house, sexual euphemisms of the time—such as the "French Treatment"—signaled that oral sex could be purchased. Performed by sex workers at the bottom of the hierarchy (remember, contemporary hygiene standards were not commonplace in this era), the French Treatment was typically associated with establishments deemed to be "the lesser houses." Some of these places were included in the guides with far from favorable reviews—and sometimes with warnings. The house at 48 Leonard Street, Miss (Julia) Brown's— once one of the most celebrated madams in the 1830s—was described as follows: "The old bawd is on her last legs. Her house is of the vilest character; even professional bullies are afraid to enter it. . . . No respectable girl can live with her. The boarders here are the rejected of the city."

Equally unflattering was the description of Miss Emily Everette's house at 74 Crosby Street, described as a "low sink of iniquity" where "any man who 'forks out' fifty cents, can have the whole run of the house, Miss Emily included. There is also any quantity of vermin here." And patrons of Miss Jane McCord's house at 71 Mercer noted the presence of "three or four depraved creatures, who possess not a single charm that can allure a gentleman of taste. Strangers should be cautious of their visits here. She keeps awful rot-gut liquor."

These guides, independent of good or bad reviews, provide fascinating insight into not just the sexual experience of nineteenth-century brothels, but the refreshments and ambiance, too.

Sadly, few American brothel guides remain today. Many were confiscated and destroyed by antivice squads during the latter half of the nineteenth century. But the Museum of Sex's collection of these guides—perhaps our most museum-like artifacts in terms of value and rarity—represent some of the best-preserved versions of the genre found anywhere.

The question of when and where people have sex fascinates me to this day, making me wonder how we would benefit as a society if we were to begin noting the landmarks of sex, and not just of battlefields.

Once you start looking at places for their sexual possibilities, you can never quite stop. And just in case you think I'm the only one cultivating this dirty habit, having sex in an unsanctioned location is a very popular bucket list item. (Sexual bucket list, that is.) According to a 2012 Your Tango poll of thirteen hundred people, the top twenty-five places for nonbedroom sex include public locations like rooftops, balconies, elevators, stairwells, restrooms, fitting rooms, movie theaters, hospitals, and sporting events. The Frisky's "30 Places to Do It Before You Turn 30" includes all parts of the kitchen (counter, floor, restaurant, against the refrigerator), on the desk at work, in a childhood or parents' bedroom, "on a piano à la *Pretty Woman*," at the zoo, in a tent, and under a waterfall. The taboo of a location often adds to its appeal, making churches, churchyards, and cemeteries particularly charged spaces for sexual encounters.

In 2008, a drunk couple was caught having sex in a confessional booth in a church in Cesena, Italy. Although the couple at first defended the act, saying, "We are atheists and for us, having sex in church is like doing it any other place," they eventually asked the bishop for forgiveness. The confessional booth was cleansed through a "mass of reparation" (and maybe a dose of disinfectant). In 2009, a lieutenant in the attorney general's office in South Carolina was found with an eighteen-year-old stripper at Elmwood Cemetery attempting to evade police as they surveyed the site for public sex. Sex toys and Viagra were found in the car. And in 2010, a sixty-four-year-old man was arrested at a New York cemetery for masturbating and filming the act. This might seem like unwanted information about sacred landmarks, but these stories are gems for sexual cartographers like myself.

The digital age has given a whole new dimension to exhibitionism. Acts are often caught on film by bystanders who post them for the world to see. Some of the more extreme locations that have been documented include sex at the top of the Arch Bridge in Estonia, and the clock tower at the top of the Grace Brothers building in Sydney, Australia. Film footage of Belgian politician Ilse Uyttersprot having sex on top of Navarra Castle in 2011 and footage of a couple having sex in a bathroom stall at Yankee Stadium both quickly went viral. And in 2015, a Florida couple was caught (and filmed by a grandmother whose grandchildren played nearby) having sex midday on a crowded public beach. (Their tryst eventually ended in arrest. The couple endured jail time and each is now registered as a sex offender.)

Here in New York, the Standard Hotel's glass-walled rooms are deliberately designed (at least in the minds of some) so guests can put their sexual acts on display for the 3.7 million patrons of the Highline—a converted train track turned promenade—and the bars, restaurants, and luxury shops in the neighborhood. As *New York* magazine reported on June 11, 2009: "Meatpacker Ricky Serling begins his day with a view of the hotel from the meat co-op on Little West 12th Street. 'I've seen men and women, women and women, men and men [in the windows],' he says, modestly. 'Lights, leather, chains. Everything.'" And really, no one should be surprised: during construction, the hotel posted signs that said, "We'll put up with your banging if you put up with ours."

When I travel, I try not to think about how many people have slept in the same bed I inhabit—or what they have done in it. There's been much media coverage about how unsanitary a hotel room can be. This problem is so pervasive it inspired the creation of product called the Yuckinator: The Clean Sheet Detective. It's a pocket-size black light that can be used when visiting a hotel to determine its level of cleanliness. Whereas sheets are typically laundered, comforters may not be unless a stain is visible to the naked eye. The same is true of hotel furniture. Upholstered chairs and benches are typically given a deep clean only four times a year. But even more problematic are television remotes, the gateway to one of the hotel industry's biggest cash generators: TV porn. The remote is often the last thing touched after a guest's viewing pleasure.

I came across the terminology "historical DNA" in 2011 when it was used to describe the semen of four men on the carpet of Dominique Strauss-Kahn's three-thousand-dollar-a-night hotel room. I loved this euphemistic term for seminal contamination.

Room 2806 at the Sofitel in New York has become a landmark for the sexual scandal that derailed DSK's political career in France, but it's only one in a long list of historically significant hotel rooms. As the nation's political capital, Washington, D.C., has a legacy of hotel sex scandals. The infamous room 871 at the Mayflower Hotel is where New York Governor Eliot Spitzer rendezvoused with Ashley Dupre.

Hotels are certainly a hotbed of sexual activity, but the *Mapping Sex in America* exhibition also revealed that plenty of steamy encounters occur while traveling to these various destinations. We even have phrases for these acts in our vernacular, like the "mile-high club" and "road head." Celebrities like Richard Branson and Ralph Fiennes have been implicated as members of the infamous "mile-high club." In 2011, Cathay Pacific Airlines was about to launch a large-scale advertising campaign with the slogan, "Meet the team who go the extra mile to make you feel special," just as photos of a flight attendant and a pilot having sex in the cockpit were discovered.

The *Mapping of Sex* is not for the germaphobe or the prude.

The reason I loved this project, all ick factor aside, was because it allowed people to be cartographers of their own sexual experiences—charting for history where they had been, what they had done, and whom they had done it with.

The hundreds of thousands of individuals who participated in *Mapping Sex in America* did so to be a part of history, and the curious visited the site to see what was happening on their streets or in their hometowns.

Unfortunately, a few years after *Mapping Sex in America* was launched, we had to remove this tremendously popular installation due to technical difficulties. We were certainly sad to see it go, but we never expected the outpouring of disappointment from the public. Distraught e-mails flooded my in-box:

> I need to let you know that this exhibition is not working properly. I think it is one of the Absolute BEST exhibits of its kind. I LOVE it and have for years I have even Posted on there. I was checking it out tonight and it does not show anything . . . HELP. I need to know that my next crazy exploit can be anonymously posted there for the world to see. PLEASE let me know what is happening with this and let me know that it gets fixed.

Some were upset to have lost access to the stories—free erotica—and others were disappointed that they no longer had a place to share their explicit, sometimes embellished, experiences with an attentive audience. When *Mapping Sex in America* disappeared it was as if people's experiences evaporated alongside it. I don't think anyone would have been consoled if we told them that "something in the back end stopped functioning." Still, it's a technical diagnosis that makes me smile to this day.

seven

Quarter Life Crisis

I was feeling on top of the world. The grown-up life I had worked so hard to create seemed to be within my grasp. At twenty-four, I had a newly minted M.A., and had just been named curator at the Museum of Sex. I was in a great relationship that was, I believed, headed toward marriage. With the instabilities of my childhood, all I ever dreamed of was the white-picket-fence version of life.

And although there was nothing all-American about the Museum of Sex, I loved the work I was doing and the challenges it presented. Still, the past two years had taken their toll—running from the museum to grad school while trying to have a social life and maintain a long-term, long-distance relationship. Still, Nick and I were committed to each other. I believed we had a future together.

How wrong I was.

Nick and I had developed a routine of talking every morning

and texting throughout the day. It was important in our long-distance relationship to dedicate that time and be really present. Digitally present, that is. But I was starting to feel that connection weakening. After not hearing from him for a full day, I decided it was time to actually pick up the phone.

"Is everything okay there?"

"Yeah, why?" he sounded uncharacteristically distant.

"Um, I haven't heard from you since last night. And usually we don't go that long." I hated how I sounded. But there was no other way to say it.

"Look," he said. That's never a good start to a conversation with your boyfriend. "Maybe we should take a break."

I was stunned. But not so stunned as to lose my awareness. I knew what a "break" really meant and I had no interest in dancing around. "There's no break, Nick. Either we're together, or we're not together. Are you saying you want to break up?"

He said no, but he didn't sound so sure.

The distance between us grew. The phone calls became spotty. The texts practically disappeared. But when I brought up the obvious changes in our relationship, he refused to talk about it.

I decided that if he wouldn't talk on the phone, we would have the conversation in person. I booked an Amtrak ticket and went to Connecticut to surprise him. Actually, if I'm honest, I think it was more like try to convince him that we should be together. This was a conversation to have in person.

When I got to his dorm room he didn't answer, so I just let myself in as I was used to doing. Seeing his bed, his surfboard on the wall, his little coffee maker gave me a pang. This didn't feel good at all. I called him. I needed to see him immediately.

"Hey," I said.

"Hey. This isn't a great time to talk. My dad's actually visiting."

His dad was there, too?

Nick and his parents were very close, and I had become close to them as well. They had been there for me at times when my own mother was not.

"Okay. The thing is, I'm here, too."

"You're . . . where?"

"Here. In your room."

A pause.

"I'll be right there."

He showed up five minutes later and hugged me. It was comforting, but the feeling was short-lived. "Why is your dad here?"

"Honestly? Because I don't know what to do."

"To do?" I was baffled.

"Yeah. About us."

I couldn't believe my timing. Nick was clearly making some big decisions about us, and planning to do so without even talking to me.

"Where is all of this coming from?" I asked.

"Look, I love you, Sarah, I do. But I'm still finishing up college. I don't know if I can start the rest of my life right this minute."

"We want the same things . . . ," I said.

"Do we?"

"Yes!" I said adamantly. "That's why we've been together all this time when most relationships wouldn't have made it past that first summer."

But was this true? Maybe it was because I was part-time at the museum, part-time at school, and part-time with Nick that things had trickled along. I'd compartmentalized my life so everything fit, just so. Likely if we'd been in the same city, this conversation would have happened much sooner. Maybe if we'd met later in life, we would have segued into an engagement. But in that moment, the why of it didn't matter. I wanted things to work. Blind to reality, I fully believed we should be taking our relationship to the next level.

He didn't see things that way. Not at all. And it became clear, after hours of talking and tears, that there was nothing I could do to change his mind.

"I guess this is good-bye then," I said.

"I guess so," he said, regretful. As if this whole thing were my idea.

I left his room sobbing.

I was so devastated that I couldn't think straight. The logistics of taking the train back to New York felt completely overwhelming so when I spotted a taxi on campus, I hailed it like the New Yorker that I am. Crying hysterically, I took that cab from New London, Connecticut, to Manhattan. It cost me two hundred dollars. (That's a lot of grocery money for a broke graduate student.)

→◆ ◆←

It was official. I was a single, twenty-four-year-old museum curator. And on my agenda: porn, porn, and more porn.

After the success of *Stags, Smokers and Blue Movies,* we saw how strongly our patrons responded to sex on film, in a museum. The success of that exhibition could easily be attributed to the content. The billion-dollar industry proved that people love porn and consume it in extraordinary quantities. But there was more to it than that. In 2005, the screen was becoming something of an extension of ourselves—something that we both looked at and projected onto in a way the world had never before experienced. It was this understanding that brought me to the first exhibition I curated on my own, *Action: Sex and the Moving Image.*

A comprehensive look at the history of sex in film, both in mainstream and pornographic films, *Action: Sex and the Moving Image* was designed to show the genealogy and evolution of society's obsession with sex through this incredible medium—a synergy of both technology and pop culture. Once very explicit in its early days and in less formal channels, sex on-screen became increasingly censored until the late 1960s/early 1970s, when the birth of the porn industry created a completely new genre of content. I wanted *Action: Sex and the Moving Image* to feel overwhelming, to mimic how inundated we are with sexual content on a daily basis.

To put the exhibition together, I had to spend hours upon hours watching and editing porn, looking for that exhibition-worthy moment—something aside from all the monotonous, jackhammer sex. Inevitably, during this period, I could be found in the conference room, remote in hand, eyes glazed from looking at hard-core sex for so many hours. The whole process became so tedious at times that I would watch it all on fast-forward, whizzing through the predictable gang bangs and deep throat scenes, desperate to find something unique. I felt like I was skimming through a book for that one thing worth quoting. It was a unique exercise in training my curatorial eye, to say the very least.

But while much of the content followed the same patterns, pace, and aesthetics, during my hours of watching porn for the exhibition, I was also exposed to all of the niches—the true spectrum—of what people were doing on-screen. And that's what I wanted the exhibition to mirror: just how overwhelmed I felt by all of this material.

Explicit depictions of sex can be challenging in any medium, but film is a uniquely heightened experience that allows viewers to act as voyeurs and derive pleasure from the desire, pain, and excitement featured on-screen.

Mainstream filmmaking began as an unregulated playground, where sexual images and themes were not only notably present but shockingly explicit, particularly at the beginning of the twentieth century. Often, sex in film was treated as a humorous part of life, taking the form of a risqué joke or amorous scene.

But over time, public concern about its social purpose and impact increased, particularly as early filmmakers continued pushing boundaries in their depictions of sex.

In 1930, the MPPDA (Motion Picture Producers and Distributors of America) created the Motion Picture Production Code, which outlined exactly what should and should not appear on-screen, regulating depictions of crime, sex, profanity, and a range of other topics perceived to challenge American ideals of upright living and "good taste."

The code cracked down on sex in many forms. It forbade nudity, white slavery (prostitution and sex trafficking of white women), miscegenation (sex between different races), sex perversion (anything that wasn't considered traditionally heterosexual), and scenes of childbirth, among other topics.

Following the institution of the code, if sex was discussed or addressed in film, it was usually condemned, or negatively portrayed through figures like the hypersexualized male foreigner, the divorced woman, or the "vampire" or "vamp," an immoral, desirous woman who ruined the lives of men.

Sex in the cinema was, thus, forced beneath the surface during this so-called Golden Age of Hollywood.

Although compliance to the Production Code was voluntary, a film's commercial success depended upon conformity. To have their works distributed to major theaters, filmmakers were forced to abide by these standards. But many found a way around the strict rules, using subtler means, like metaphor, innuendo, and humor, to communicate. Instead of showing sex acts explicitly, symbolic imagery—such as trains going through tunnels—were used as a substitute.

Similarly, food was frequently used to suggest sex on-screen. These shrouded versions of oral sex focus on the sensual experiences of "tasting" and "consuming."

As a result of all this repression, two marginal markets for film developed: the stag films (those stalwarts of the bachelor party) and the "exploitation" genre. An exploitation film is generally a low-budget movie that focuses on a current trend, a niche genre, or a provocative or lurid subject matter—what we generally think of as B movies. *Reefer Madness* is the best example. A scare-tactic film that promoted the notion that smoking "reefer" would cause the downfall of society and lead to violence, *Reefer Madness* not only played on societal fears related to youth culture, it escalated them.

Within the exploitation genre are several subgenres, "sexploitation" being one of the most popular. Sexploitation films are just what they sound like: films that use sexual content to make them commercially appealing. These movies had the pretense of being real films—that is to say, they had something of a plot; nevertheless, they were largely an excuse to show as much nudity as possible.

Early sexploitation films highlighted sexuality by depicting perceived social ills, like premarital sex and prostitution. As the genre progressed, it took on a wide variety of forms, from nudist films to "nudie cuties" to "Mondo" documentaries. Nudie cuties are films that do not include sexual acts or simulated sex. They rely on nude depictions of the body, like those of burlesque films, for their appeal. Nudie cuties are completely camp and have large-breasted, topless women, for no real reason. Mondo films were fake documentaries that typically focused on foreign cultures and depicted them as either hypersexual (the eroticized *National Geographic* feel) or savages. Mondo films intertwined sexploitation with racist sentiment.

Mild-mannered, nudist films became a part of the "sexploitation" genre because they were among the first in the United States to expose the nude body on-screen. *Elysia* (1933) is considered the first nudist film, but the genre did not become popular until the 1954 release of *Garden of Eden.* The success of this film sparked legal controversy in 1957, when it was ruled that the depiction of nudity in itself was not obscene.

Hollywood was liberated in 1968 when the Production Code was finally replaced with the Motion Picture Association of America's rating system—the scale we know today as the ratings G (General Audiences), M (Mature Audiences), R (Restricted), and X (persons under eighteen not admitted). Curiously, the only X-rated film ever to win an Academy Award was *Midnight Cowboy* in 1969, a story about a male sex worker.

It was Linda Lovelace, the star of *Deep Throat,* who became the first porn star. Linda appeared on the cover of *Esquire* and attended prestigious events like the Academy Awards, becoming the girl everyone wanted to be seen with *and* the girl that everyone wanted to have sex with. Linda's newfound celebrity brought her face-to-face with cinematic and musical legends. She was even flown to the Playboy Mansion to party with Hugh Hefner, whom she later described as "the best ass-fuck I've ever had."* And according to Sammy Davis Jr., in 1973, "The biggest status symbol this year is to have your cock sucked by Linda Lovelace."†

Of all the hours of porn I watched, the most memorable—in that way you wish you could unsee it—was Linda Lovelace having sex with a dog. That was in *Dog Fucker* (1971), a film she denied ever having made. There are many theories about why she denied it. Maybe she was ashamed of it. Maybe she didn't do it willingly. Maybe she was worried it would ruin her career? (It was filmed the year before her *Deep Throat* fame.) Who knows. We did not show the Linda Lovelace bestiality footage, nor do we ever show footage between nonconsenting partners.

Although some of the content I viewed for the exhibition was very difficult to watch, I needed to view it as objectively as possible. I needed to observe the material as an artifact of sexuality and a mirror to our evolving societal attitudes toward sex. *Action: Sex in the Moving Image* wasn't about taking a position on porn, nor was it about glamorizing or demonizing it. The exhibition set out to explain and contextualize the material, which is why curatorial text scrolled at the bottom of the monitor for every one of the more than two hundred films presented. No matter your thoughts on the impact and value of porn, one thing we can't do is pretend it doesn't exist.

---

* Legs McNeil and Jennifer Osborne, *The Other Hollywood: The Uncensored Oral History of the Porn Film Industry* (New York: It Books, 2005), p. 103.

† Darwin Porter, *Inside Linda Lovelace's Deep Throat: Degradation, Porno Chic, and the Rise of Feminism* (New York: Blood Moon Productions, 2013), p. i.

eight

The Power of the
Erotic Imagination

Each day I spent hour upon hour watching porn. And nearly every night of the week, I went out with friends, trying to get over my heartache for Nick. Whatever the cool bar/club of the moment was—Pink Elephant, Cain, PM—you name it, I was there. And if a bouncer wouldn't let me in, there was always my Museum of Sex business card. That usually did the trick.

I had been with Nick for nearly three years and my heart needed to do some serious healing. It felt good to be a little irresponsible. Just to be a regular twentysomething living in New York City. I'd been working so hard to balance full-time graduate school, my position at the museum, and a long-distance relationship, but now that my relationship had ended I was finally able to admit to myself what a strain it had been to keep it all together. And even though I knew I wanted marriage and children (what people refer to euphemistically as "settling down"), I also knew that, at twenty-four, I had time. So I bought a "freedom dress" at American Apparel—a skin-tight plum tube dress—and wore it as if it were the uniform of my new single status.

The trendy clubs were a great distraction. But they also gave me a dismal view of dating in NYC. Meeting men in that setting, I saw how they didn't take me seriously—especially when I told them I worked at the Museum of Sex. With my business card and my freedom dress, I was perceived as a promiscuous party girl, when that wasn't me at all.

It's no wonder I attracted one of Manhattan's most famous womanizers.

I had been waiting for a cab in the Meatpacking District when a man came up to me and said, "I had to let you know you are so beautiful."

I thanked him, then promptly turned away, as if hailing a cab were the most important thing I would do that day. Undeterred, he continued. I was impressed by his confidence and, if I'm honest, his compliments came at a time I needed them. I guess that's why I gave him my number. He was good-looking, with dark hair and brown eyes—and I thought, *why not?* He called a few days later and I agreed to meet him at a bar on the East Side.

Paul was better looking than I remembered. He was funny and clearly intelligent. Not seeing any immediate red flags, I began to relax as he ordered us drinks. But that changed quickly.

"So what do you do?" he asked me.

"Guess," I told him. This, along with guessing my heritage, both impossible for people to determine, had become a fun game my girlfriends liked to play on a night out.

"You're a publicist," he said. I shook my head. "You . . . have a blog. About fashion." No. His guesses moved increasingly further away from anything remotely related to my field of interest. That's why, when it came time to tell him my real job, I was excited to share the big reveal. I shouldn't have been. No sooner were the words "I work at the Museum of Sex" out of my mouth than his hands were all over me. And I mean *all over me*.

His less-than-gentlemanly approach and dramatic X-rated turn in the conversation made me realize I needed to quickly extricate myself from this situation. Disturbed and disappointed, I chalked it up to just another dating fail for the women of New York City.

A few days later, he e-mailed me. I naively imagined it was an apology waiting in my in-box. But he didn't acknowledge his groping or the way I ran out of the bar. In fact, it wasn't an apology that he had in mind—it was an invitation. An invitation to a *sex* party.

Paul wasn't the first man to make assumptions because of my job, and he wouldn't be the last. But he was one of the most persistent. I had always thought that people like Paul Janka were urban legends, like the Coke and Pop Rocks myth, or the alligator in the sewer. Not so. Although I wouldn't be aware of this until years later, Paul was the author of a seventeen-page manifesto called "Getting Laid in NYC: Technology for the Single Man."

Paul claims to have always been fascinated by women and sex, a hobby, he says, to which he devotes "considerable time and effort." Paul's manifesto is full of gems, including this one: "You are never 'bothering' a girl by hitting on her. Remember that it's your duty as a man to engage the opposite sex and initiate contact. Don't get into thinking you're being intrusive. She will let you know."

But this fascination also swung darker. Way darker. Janka's

manifesto also describes how he recommends making arrangements with bartenders to serve the man on the make plain tonic (instead of the vodka tonic he appears to order) while simultaneously serving his date whatever alcoholic beverage she requested. Janka's date would believe that he was drinking steadily alongside her, but in reality he was doing what he could to ensure that she was feeling relaxed while he remained sober so that he could get her into his bed. Clearly, this skewed version of dating and seduction had some serious issues to work through.

Navigating the dating scene is difficult for everyone, but when you work at the Museum of Sex you do tend to attract more than your fair share of . . . undesirables. In this case a man who would later be in consideration for Gawker's Douche of the Decade title. Paul continued to contact me in the coming weeks, texting me at all hours of the day and night, even going so far as to call me on different cell phones so that I wouldn't recognize his number. While I could pretend it was because he saw something special in me, in reality I was just another woman, one of many, on the late-night booty call list. He was a telemarketer of sex, and when I told him I'd be calling the police if I got another call, he heeded my warning.

So, as far as Janka's advice goes: "Don't get into thinking you're being intrusive. She will let you know." I guess you could say *I let him know.*

→◆ ◆←

"This is our next exhibition," Dan said, dropping a copy of *Deviant Desires: Incredibly Strange Sex* by Katharine Gates on my desk.

I was familiar with Katharine Gates. She too had studied anthropology, and her book, published in 2000, had become an underground cult classic. The mainstream took notice when George Gurley featured her in his *Vanity Fair* article "Pleasures of the Fur," which was about furries, "people whose interest in animal characters goes further than an appreciation of *The Lion King*." (Essentially, furries are a subculture of people who wear anthropomorphized fur animal costumes, or "fursuits," at times engaging in sexual situations.) Dan took notice when he and John went to Katharine's lecture at New York University. And when Dan and John took notice of something, that something became a priority.

Whereas a concept in the traditional museum world could take ten years or more to execute, this wasn't the case at MoSex. We didn't have any red tape to cut, no hoops to jump through. The road from idea to exhibition was often short—and could be very bumpy.

So when the Katharine Gates inspiration hit, it was full steam ahead with *Kink: The Geography of the Erotic Imagination*. But where to even begin? How do you talk about all of the things that can be erotic, when almost anything can be erotic for someone? If sex is a tremendous topic for one little museum to cover, then kink, in all of its vastness, might be considered at the core.

Fortunately, not only was the exhibition based on a book, but we were working directly with the author. An artist-anthropologist, Katharine had actually created a map of the world of kink in which she visually represented the connections and overlap between various kink communities. From fantasies and desires often rooted in the fetishization of various materials such as latex, leather, and fur, to impulses, such as transformation, control, and taboo, Katharine's map served as the jumping-off point in the exploration of the "geography" of the erotic imagination.

Here we had a strong organizing principle, a primary resource, and a clear starting point. I read *Deviant Desires* again and again, eager to immerse myself in Katharine's perspective on the topic. Unlike past projects where I had to research collectors and experts, this time I had Katharine's network to get things started. She'd spent years reaching out to people in the kink and fetish communities, befriending and gaining their trust, establishing an eclectic network of contacts. Still, there was a great deal of legwork involved because it had been close to a decade since some of these connections had been made. (Not only do people move and change their e-mail address, but sometimes they change their kinks.)

Kink was a different kind of exhibition for me, and for the museum. Until this point, much of my work had been standard curatorial assignments, sharing unknown histories through fine art, photography, and film. But this was the first time I'd been asked to look deeper into a subject and translate the psychology of artifacts, to ask why the objects had been created in the first place. What inspired a particular kink? How had the kink evolved and how was it communicated to intimate partners? It wasn't just about the biography of a particular artifact or kink, it was about providing explanations of *why* the objects were made and how they were used. It required a whole new way to think about sex, and in this case, a whole new way to interact with the artists and lenders whose work was featured in the exhibition.

Artists, independent of their medium or genre, are passionate people. With strong opinions about how their work should be displayed and the conversation that should surround it, they sometimes come into conflict with curators. (Nowhere is this more evident than in the "official value" of a particular work. An artist can be reluctant to understand that the insurance company needs a little more to go on than the artist's notion that his or her art is worth a million dollars.) A good curator must be understanding and patient. He or she must be open and must listen closely, especially when the artist's work is engaged in a sensitive topic such as sex, and when that work involves the artist's own sexuality. You can have all the academic training in the world, but if you can't be sensitive to different types of people, you won't be able to do this kind of work.

Working on *Kink* didn't change me as a curator as much as it made me realize that I possessed a natural desire to want to listen and learn from people—a skill that would prove invaluable throughout the course of the exhibition. But there was a learning curve, one that required a genuine understanding of the concept of "kink."

The terms *fetish* and *kink* are often used interchangeably, but there's an important distinction to be made: A fetish is something required for sexual excitement and release, whereas a kink is an addition to or enhancement of sexual pleasure. A kink isn't mandatory—it just heightens the experience.

Katharine's book was invaluable in explaining each particular kink/fetish and translating how an act becomes a turn-on.

Kinks can take any form, really. Some are tied to a preference for certain types of clothing such as high heels, corsets, stockings, or military uniforms. Wristwatches and angora sweaters really do it for some people. Other kinks are for particular parts of the body like breasts or the nape of the neck. Oral fixations abound. For some, watching others smoke, eat, chew gum, or suck on a lollipop is deeply erotic.

Other kinks are rooted in transformation fantasies in which

the individuals are endowed with some kind of fantastical power. By becoming something otherworldly, like a vampire or animal (pony play represents one of the largest kink communities in the United States and the United Kingdom), the individual is given the freedom of uninhibited sexual expression. Others desire more submissive fantasies, like being turned into a robot or a doll— even human furniture, where the body is folded, bound, and formed into utilitarian objects like chairs, coffee tables, and lamps. These kinks are just as much about transformation as they are about relinquishing control. In these new roles, transformation kinksters can let societal expectations slide away.

Some kinks are about breaking taboos. In a culture that puts cleanliness next to godliness, it can be freeing and potentially exciting for some to see a face covered in pie (pie play) or a clothed body splashed with water (wetlook), revealing hints of newly exposed skin peeking through. Sploshing enthusiasts are turned on by bodies covered in paint, mud (mudlarkers), food products (whipped cream, condiments, and chocolate sauce are popular), and even bodily fluids, such as semen, urine, feces, and blood. Fantasies about sexually ravenous nuns, Lolitas, and nonconsenting partners also fall within these kinks of taboo. And for others, being "bad" is the emotional thrill that transforms sex.

Some kinks are essentially metaphors of arousal and climax. The fantasy is often about a process intensifying, almost pulsating with the unknown, such as watching someone blow up a balloon, watching it get bigger and bigger as the latex thins and tightens, waiting for the outcome, the eventual . . . POP. For "looners"— people with a balloon kink—seeing this symbolic climax triggers an actual orgasm. Fireworks, bombs, breaking dishes, popping zits, and plastic bags can all represent a similar orgasmic explosion.

Another kink niche: cake farts. For some, a video of a barely clothed woman hovering her backside over a cake and coyly whispering, "Know what I like the most? Cake farts. . . . Um, let's get this done," then passing gas over the confection, is equivalent to watching Jenna Jameson in an orgy. Like I said, everything and anything can be a kink for someone.

In another amazing example, one man's ultimate fantasy was to be a turkey cooked at Thanksgiving dinner. He got inside an imaginary oven (a cardboard box) and paid a woman to say things such as, "I'm turning up the temperature," "It's getting hotter and hotter," "I'm going to baste your hot juices." With only verbal encouragement, he reached orgasmic satisfaction.

→◆ ◆←

One of the first members of kink subculture I met was a man I'll call M. He was our link to the adult baby community (AB), a group of people whose fetish is regressing to a baby or toddler state, wearing baby clothes, and drinking from bottles—that sort of thing.

M was a mild-mannered man who came to the museum to drop off some of his artifacts for the exhibition, including an adult-size high chair that we were going to put on display. I gained a much better understanding of the AB world through M, who patiently described how most ABs are men who like to dress like little girls, often commissioning specially tailored baby doll dresses and employing the services of a sitter to care for them, comfort them, at times discipline them, and, in some cases, even change their adult-size diapers.

The interactions between the sitter and the adult baby need not be directly sexual. In some cases the satisfaction is derived solely from the comfort afforded them, rather than through direct sexual stimulation. Although some sitters—or mommies, daddies, nannies, governesses, infantilizers, or sissifiers—engage in these dynamics for their own pleasure, many charge an hourly rate for their services. Some professional sitters advertise a wide selection of play items, key components for AB participants. Since the AB community varies widely in age, it's important that nuances, like having cloth and disposable diapers, are accounted for. The textures and materials of these early exposures are critical to the execution of the total fantasy.

Before his trip to the museum, M asked if he could come dressed in his preferred outdoor adult baby clothing, adult-size denim overalls and a white, long-sleeved waffle T-shirt with the letters ABC embroidered near the collar. Of course, we told him this was completely okay, and that we wanted him to feel comfortable. (We never discussed if he was or was not wearing a diaper under his clothing. I'm guessing he was.)

As we unwrapped the items for display, we chatted for a while about the exhibition and its goals. It was a perfectly average meeting in some respects, until I scanned the motley crew sitting around our conference table: M and me on one side, and on the other, Katharine, our kink expert, and in a little bassinet, Katharine's newborn.

It wasn't every day that an adult man and a baby wore similar outfits, and to the office for that matter. It was one of those moments when I really had to pause and realize how atypical my life had become.

As strange and surreal as this meeting was, I learned a great deal from our candid conversation, not just about M's specific kink, but also about how his kink shaped the rest of his life.

M described how, prior to the proliferation of chat rooms and Internet communities, he thought he was alone in his sexual desires, and this made him feel great loneliness and isolation. Times were now changing, and eventually M was able to talk about his kink to his wife. She was supportive, even converting part of their basement into a nursery. Still, she didn't want to participate as one of his sitters. This was where she put her foot down.

→⬩ ⬩←

Within the world of kink, BDSM is one of the most popular and well-known categories. The practice was originally coined S/M, for sadism and masochism, by Richard von Krafft-Ebing, a German psychiatrist and author of the 1886 work *Psychopathia Sexualis,* a foundational text in the world of sex research. Although Krafft-Ebing is credited for the terms *sadism* and *masochism,* scholarship has shown that he was simply referencing terminology used in the sexual underground by people who were familiar with the erotic literary works of Marquis de Sade and Leopold von Sacher-Masoch. By the turn of the century, with the popularization of the works of figures like Sigmund Freud, the term *sadomasochism* became well recognized in academia, creative circles, and even the mainstream.

Some attribute the proliferation of S/M or representations of BDSM kinks to Victorian representations of mother's whipping girls for discipline—between 1867 and 1874 the Englishwoman's *Domestic Magazine* featured letters of this nature—as well as the short-lived Weimar Republic that flourished in the period between the world wars, from 1918 to 1933. This intermediary stage in German history featured a thriving intellectual and art scene, one that didn't shy away from sex. Berlin became the epicenter of Freudian analysis, avant-garde cabaret and cinema, and prostitution. This burst of sexual innovation wasn't limited to Germany. In fact, it spread throughout Europe and the United Kingdom, where magazines such as *London Life* (1923–41) featured correspondence about rubber, leather, piercing, tattoos, human ponies, high heels, corsetry, amputation, and female impersonation. Eventually, BDSM traveled to America when the GIs returned home. These GIs, previously known for their naïveté, had cultivated a new desire for bondage, submission, and humiliation images.

Burgeoning erotic industries emerged to satisfy these desires. Take Irving Klaw, the owner of a small photography shop in New York City, who made a business of commodifying these new tastes. Klaw's customers desired specifically stylized photos: women engaged in bondage dynamics and spanking situations, in some cases wearing dangerously high heels and seamed stockings, perfectly straight—a new requirement for the ultimate fantasy. Irving and his sister Paula set up their own photo studio to create a product that fulfilled these sexual desires. This was the kind of content that was kept under the counter instead of out on the open magazine rack. In Klaw's studio, Bettie Page, alongside burlesque performers such as Tempest Storm, dressed in lingerie and acted out various bondage scenarios. Some images featured women bound or hogtied. Others presented groups of women wrestling and even restraining, gagging, or flogging one another. He was careful not to show actual sex acts—no kissing, intercourse, or full-on nudity.

Irving Klaw's business soon extended into filmmaking; he created the burlesque cult classics *Varietease* (1954) and *Teaserama* (1955). Despite being cautious, Klaw still found his way into a legal battle with censors. Out of fear, he decided to burn the negatives of many of the images in question. Luckily, Klaw's sister hid thousands. Without her intervention, Bettie Page would have been erased from history.

→✦ ✦←

The final exhibition of *Kink: The Geography of the Erotic Imagination* had photos, drawings, and objects that represent the wide ranges of kinks and fetishes. One woman lent us her saddle and bridle for pony play. Someone else provided us with an inflation suit that looked like a body bag. For cannibal play we had photographs from Muki's Kitchen, an assortment of beautiful women stylized and presented like the succulent dishes of Michelin star restaurants. An oversize platter with fruit all around was created so people could lie down and take photos as if they were the edible centerpiece. It was an exhibition not just about learning, but participation and exploration. Then there was a whole medical play setup, including a table and tools where visitors could put on a nurse hat and handle all the instruments medical play enthusiasts might use. The exhibition encouraged dress-up. Patrons could try on a wolf-head mask created for us by a member of the furry community, and a female latex mask used by members of a community interested in experiencing what it's like to be in the skin of a woman.

No one who experienced the exhibition would ever think of the terms *kink* or *fetish* in a vague, abstract way ever again. Me included. Not only did staging this exhibition give me access to people's wide range of sexual predilections, but it showed me how open communication about kinks and fetishes can strengthen relationships. Consider the tremendous honesty it took for M and his wife to understand and respect each other, and how they were able to overcome what could have been a deeply destructive lack of communication. Many people believe that, because members of the BDSM community traverse such complicated physical and emotional terrain, their interpersonal dynamics are stronger and healthier than those of more conventional sexual relationships. More than inspiring new sexual fantasies, this was my personal takeaway from the research I was doing. The thing I wanted to apply and absorb into my own life.

With my newfound awareness and understanding of the kink community, I found it hard to believe that these desires were once considered paraphilias, or mental disorders, by psychologists. Even homosexuality was considered a paraphilia as recently as 1973.

Support communities are a relatively new phenomenon, and before the Internet, many kinksters, like M, not only felt completely alone but also thought they were sick or perverted. This "scientific" take on sexuality, combined with moral judgments and legal restrictions, proved deeply destructive to generations of people. Today, many preferences once considered paraphilias—such as sodomy and role play—are accepted in the mainstream. But while society has become more accepting, some kinks, like rape fantasies, necrophilia, and bestiality, remain taboo.

Some of the kinks and fetishes we came across pushed personal boundaries. Everyone, including those of us who work at the Museum of Sex, have their personal limits. For me, it was vomit porn. (I'm one of those people who can't watch others get sick.) For Mark, one of my closest friends and colleagues, it was a particular strain of forniphilia.

Forniphilia is human furniture play in which a person is

bound, shaped, and used as an inanimate object like a chair or table. For instance, a woman could be bound on all fours, with her back used as a tabletop on which the master eats his dinner. This relinquishing of complete control and power to the dominant is, for some, a tremendous turn-on. No physical stimulation or penetration is required.

"Let me know what you think," I said, sending him the link. "It's mostly erotica and fantasy, but a few of the contributors have made some interesting art. There might be something exhibition-worthy in there."

Mark clicked on the site, and after a few minutes he blurted, "I just came across my worst nightmare: a woman consenting to being trapped in a box, buried underground for the rest of her life, kept alive through feeding tubes and colostomy bags." All traces of her humanness were removed, even her eyelashes. She was now just a "thing" to be controlled by the whims of the dominant.

Although deeply unnerving to Mark, this type of fantasy is highly erotic for others—proving there is no one-size-fits-all version of eroticism and sexuality. And this was the point of the exhibition: the diversity of the erotic imagination is truly infinite. It wasn't that we were trying to transform everyone into a kinkster. Instead, we were trying to shed light on how sex and imagination can be both one and the same and separate. And fantasy is not always the same as reality.

Working on *Kink* opened my eyes to a whole world of sexual desire. And, in the end, it transformed my understanding of sex. I now believe that, when shared among consenting adults, kink is an outlet for adult play, and, dare I say, fun.

nine

Sarah Sex

Once I knew that every little thing I did throughout the day could be fetishized—dangling my shoe, blowing a bubble with my gum, exposing the nape of my neck—I couldn't stop thinking about it. Spending the last few months surrounded by kink, I was now hyperaware that just about anything could be a turn-on. It was becoming impossible for me to leave work at the office.

I had a new awareness of people. Especially men. If I met a guy, I couldn't help but wonder what his "thing" was. And it wasn't a question of whether he had a "thing." They all did. Or so I was convinced.

One night in October, tired of wallowing over Nick, I put on my freedom dress and cajoled my friend Diana into going out with me to a party. It was the birthday party of a friend of a friend, and I knew this particular group of people would ensure we were out way past last call, likely until the sun came out. Just what I was in the mood for.

After our pregame ritual of applying too much blush and eyeliner (and drinking overly strong cocktails in my apartment), Diana and I had time to kill before the party. To keep up the distractions, we stopped by Cain, a taxi garage turned popular club that, according to the *New York Post,* offered "more celebrity sightings than the Betty Ford clinic." After Cain we moved on to G-Lounge, which that evening happened to be filled with sketchy, older Russian men. (Not exactly inspiring for a woman who had just ended a relationship with the man she thought she'd marry.) Looking around at G-Lounge, at the men old enough to be my father, the men who thought that buying a drink meant an invitation to bed, and the men who looked like they spent more time on their looks than I did, I was terrified that I was glimpsing my future. That was it. That and the influence of those supersweet cocktails from earlier. I burst into tears in the lobby of the Gansevoort Hotel. I was convinced that I'd be alone forever. And with those choices, maybe it was for the best.

By the time Diana and I showed up at Babel, all I wanted to do was go home and crawl into bed. But I was nothing if not resilient, so I made my way through the dark and narrow Middle-Eastern-meets-Reggae bar to wish our friend Eyas a happy birthday. That's when I locked eyes with his friend, a Nigel Barker lookalike who really could be described as tall, dark, and handsome. As if that weren't enough, when he smiled at me, I felt something. Instant attraction.

As we tried to introduce ourselves over the bass, I could hear an accent. It was different from the rest of the group, mostly Saudis and Moroccans, many of whom had met at American colleges and had further bonded at every house music venue across New York City. As he leaned down to tell me his name—Mahir—I tried to size up how old he was. Given that the rest of the crowd was typically a handful of years older than I was, I guessed thirty.

Mahir took my hand and led me to the middle of the congested dance floor. (Quite a change from the typical guy who needed to be forced to dance.) We were packed in tightly, which prevented anything like a polite distance between our bodies. Our hips moved together, hitting every beat no matter how fast. We stayed together like that until the end of the night. Other than the fact that our bodies moved to the same rhythm, we knew very little about each other. Still, as we stumbled out with the crowd onto Avenue C, we exchanged numbers.

To my surprise, Mahir texted me the next day—which my girlfriends confirmed was practically a sin for a single man in NYC. We made arrangements for an after-work school-night date. Work that day consisting of: thinking through bondage restraints and how best to display them; talking with the exhibition designers about where would we put that life-size masked leather cupid cutout—paddle in hand—so that it would be the perfect greeting for visitors as they entered the gallery. (Kinky, yes, but the opposite of intimidating for patrons who might be shocked by the rest of the gallery.)

I may have been a woman with nipple clamps on my desk, but that didn't make me any less nervous for the date.

After work I met Mahir at a loungy restaurant on the West Side. I was nervous. It can be awkward to meet up with someone again after a drunken night out. They're often not quite as good-looking as you remember. After enough drinks my Nigel Barker could easily have been closer to Bob Barker. (Beer goggles aren't the sole domain of men.) I was worried that the conversation might be stilted, or that the person I was wildly attracted to seemed like some sort of dream.

So I was relieved when Mahir was exactly as I remembered him. Without the music of the club, we were finally able to connect over more than just our dancing. As we learned about each other (at least the date version of our life stories), I think we both felt that the connection was undeniable.

Ethnically Palestinian, Mahir had grown up in Kuwait and had been smuggled as a small child into Jordan when the nation was no longer safe. As we talked and talked—and as I was about to start my third glass of wine—I noticed that Mahir never ordered a drink. Should I be wary? Was he one of those guys who stays sober just to get a woman loaded and take advantage of her? I'd had brush-ins with that type already and while I didn't really think that was the case for Mahir, I had to call him on it, for peace of mind, if nothing else.

"I don't drink alcohol," he said.

"Oh. Sorry. I didn't mean to bring up a delicate topic." I hadn't noticed he was sober the other night at Babel—probably because I was drunk. Maybe he was in recovery like a number of people I'd known.

"It's no big deal. I'm Muslim, and I try to follow my faith as best I can."

Having partied with the same group of friends for years, many of whom had been sneaking me into bars since I was nineteen, I hadn't encountered this before. I had known people who had grown up with more traditional and conservative backgrounds (no matter their religious affiliations), a great many of whom had decided to lead separate social lives here in New York. There was an unspoken understanding that here in the city they would be fun-loving adults, no different from any American postgrad, and that they would at some point return to their home nations/communities and a completely different trajectory. I wondered how religious Mahir was, and what this would mean.

Although it didn't matter to me, I could only imagine what my Jewish grandmother would say about this new suitor. But she also hadn't been thrilled when my mother had brought home my dark-skinned Mexican American father. Or when my *abuela* would feed me *nopales,* horrifying my maternal grandmother that her granddaughter was eating cactus. We were of different generations and sensibilities. But since Mahir didn't seem to have a problem being out with a girl whose last name was Jacobs, why should I?

Then he asked about my job.

"My job," I said, looking into the dark, beautiful eyes of my date who didn't indulge in alcohol. "I work at a museum."

"Really? MoMa? The Guggenheim?"

"No. The Museum of Sex."

I waited for him to be shocked or turned off, but he seemed to find it interesting. Mahir wasn't just handsome, but brilliant. An MIT graduate, he was just as nerdy as I was, if not a little bit more. We had a terrific date. At the end of the night, he walked me to a cab, but before I got in he grabbed me and kissed me. And it was a great kiss.

Mahir started texting me every day. His texts were so frequent, I found it hard to keep up. (It was in an archaic time when I didn't have a smartphone.) But while he lavished attention on me, even bringing me chicken soup when I was home one day with a terrible cold, something about the dynamic made me feel that all of it was on his terms. Still, I couldn't help myself. He was, quite simply, sweeping me off my feet.

In many ways Mahir seemed like the unicorn of New York City dating stories; nevertheless, there were warning signs. Although everything felt intense and passionate, I was always aware that he wasn't my boyfriend, nor was I his girlfriend, even though I found my way to his apartment at the end of most of my crazy nights out (a homebody, he was happier staying in watching movies and playing video games). This all took place between the lines: not being introduced to his brothers who lived in the city; the fact that we spent most of our time in his apartment, instead of out with friends. As close and communicative as we seemed, it was clear that certain parts of his life were off limits to me.

My friends would tell me, "Sarah, you realize this is *never* going to happen." They would remind me that I wasn't the good Middle Eastern girl he was expected to be with. Oh, and that my job rendered me entirely unsuitable for an observant Muslim family. But if Mahir didn't want to admit these were obstacles, neither did I. So I continued with our complex courtship as I continued with my complex and kinky exhibition.

→◆ ◆←

During my many viewings of the film *Willy Wonka and the Chocolate Factory* as a kid, I never suspected that Violet Beauregarde was a sex icon.

If you recall, Violet's folly of eating the forbidden Wonka gum leads her to expand to fantastical proportions, basically turning her into a gigantic blueberry. She is only saved by being "juiced." Believe it or not, this kind of expansion and "juicing" is a widespread fantasy, signifying a kind of arousal and release.

Of course, real bodies can't expand in the way that Violet's did, but kink illustrators have long tried to capture this concept of spontaneous growth and expansion for their followers. While today women can get breast augmentations of astonishing proportions—check out Busty Dusty and her 90HHH cups, Minka at 52KKK, Beshine at a Z cup, and Keisha Evans whose breasts are so large they are uncategorizable—there was a time when this sort of extreme physicality simply couldn't exist in reality. But through an illustrator's pencil, the fantasy could be brought to life.

Learning about this particular community shed light on drawings in the museum's permanent collection. Mysterious and compelling, this artwork is lovingly referred to as the "big bottom girls." A collection of one hundred double-sided drawings portraying BDSM fantasies and focusing on women with exaggerated posteriors, these big bottom girls were found abandoned in a briefcase in an apartment in Denmark. The images feature a series of recurring characters dressed in turn-of-the-century Scandinavian peasant garb. In many, an older gentleman with round wire-frame glasses ties down the big bottom girls and aggressively spanks them, making their bottoms glow hues of red and purple. One or two of the drawings have the scribblings of an erotic narrative in the margins. The artist is unknown, and the only clue to the origin of the collection is a Maersk shipping slip on which one of the drawings was completed. It dates back to Denmark in the 1960s.

Today, kinksters don't have to rely on mere drawings of their fantasy form. We now have methods for actually inflating the body or mimicking the experience. There are latex and rubber suits that can be pumped full with air to inflate specific parts or the whole body, depending on the user's fantasy. In addition to inflation, it is also the sensation of confinement and bondage within that's titillating.

Although inflation allows for immediate results, it's not everyone's fantasy. Another group sexualizes the slow physical growth associated with pregnancy (often accompanied by a lactation kink/fetish), as well as the gradual growth of eroticized weight gain. This is the root of the feeder/gainer fantasy. Gainers get off on their own bodies growing to gigantic proportions through the consumption of a near-obscene number of calories. Feeders are stimulated by the idea of being the enabler of these gains. The ultimate expression of the kink manifests when the gainers become so large they can no longer care for themselves and become dependent on their feeder. For both, the consumption of food is erotic, as is the subsequent measuring and weighing.

Creativity is limitless when it comes to crafting the needed props to realize a wide assortment of other sexual fantasies. One exhibition lender, Ron, used his creativity and craft skills to actualize his kink. An unusually polite guy with a gentle disposition, Ron has a kink for giantesses and actually creates mini cardboard cities for the sole purpose of being stepped on by real-life women. Ron lies on the floor next to his minicities while average-size women demolish the landscapes. From Ron's prone perspective, these women appear as if they are his idealized female figure—the giantess.

Ron finds that this kink permits him to create an alternative reality for himself. He gets to embody a different physical and emotional space. As Katharine writes in her book, "Ron feels that the giantess is not only a mother figure, but also an alter-ego, a part of himself that is permitted to be angry." In addition to his miniature sets, Ron—who is African American—creates collages depicting his giantess fantasies. These images, which focus on African American women with supersize power, are featured in his publication *Black Giantess,* which is an extension of a fantasy hinging on the empowerment of African American women. According to Ron, "The way I perceive it is that the black female has been oppressed and taken advantage of and used so much over the centuries. . . . What would happen if she were able to get back at all of those who caused her problems? And it's a sexual thing because then she could do whatever she wanted to do, as long as she gratifies herself."

The fantasies of macrogynophiles and giantessophiles often include the idea of being smothered or crushed. These sensations also appeal to some feeders. The movies *Alice in Wonderland* and *Honey, I Shrunk the Kids* resonate because they explore the idea of the microindividual, defenseless against the gigantic, godlike human figure. Human figurines are common props for giantessophiles eager to watch the crushing of their fantasy.

The object being crushed doesn't always have to be a person. Some people get off on the idea of pumping the gas pedal, seeing cars stuck in the mud, or watching a car crash. That fetish/kink space became the basis for the 1996 film *Crash,* starring James Spader and Holly Hunter.

Other "crush freaks" want to see an insect or small animal crushed, typically by a woman who is barefoot or, alternatively, wearing very high heels. Many crush freaks imagine being that creature, with the bodily fluids released mirroring their ejaculations or orgasms. In September 2015, a Houston woman became the first to be arrested for the production of crush porn via the

Animal Crush Video Prohibition Act, which criminalizes inter-state commerce of material depicting animal torture.

For a long time, kinksters had to be industrious and secretive to get the equipment to facilitate their fantasies. If you wanted bondage equipment, you needed to make it yourself or find a trusted leathersmith. If you wanted a pair of ballet boots, you needed to find a willing shoemaker. What would a cosplay prac-titioner, furvert, or latex mask fetishist be without these items? How could a plushie bring their fantasies to life without a specially modified stuffed animal? Believe it or not, you can now find pat-terns online for creating a vagina or penis for your stuffed animal.

Locating these items was once very difficult. In the past, pur-chasing kink-related items was the terrain of the bold. People were forced to test out the receptiveness of small specialty shops. For some of these businesses, understanding the desires of their customers had entrepreneurial rewards. Such was the case for high-end lingerie boutiques when they realized that a growing percentage of their male clients were requesting items in sizes that mirrored their own proportions rather than their wives'.

One such business, the Michael Salem Boutique, has been ca-tering to the cross-dressing, trans, and drag communities since the early 1900s. This family business, originally known as Salem Hosiery, caters to not only men seeking to wear women's cloth-ing but also those looking for items to help fill out feminine curves and hide masculine appendages. Over the years it has become the go-to place for men seeking women's clothing. Michael Salem's *How to Impersonate a Woman*—book and video—is said to have been used by director Beeban Kidron during the shooting of the 1995 film *To Wong Foo, Thanks for Everything! Julie Newmar,* about three New York drag queens on a road trip.

The clothing and accessories sold at places like the Michael Salem Boutique aren't just about sex; they're about helping individuals feel more confident and at home in their skin. Similarly, the Museum of Sex is intended to be a safe space where identities are celebrated and protected. I can only hope that our business proves as timeless as that of the boutique.

—→◆ ◆←—

Kink: The Geography of the Erotic Imagination opened with an extravagant party: some five hundred people spilled into every room on every floor of the museum. Michael Musto from *The Village Voice* attended, as well as journalists from *The New York Times* and actor Alan Cumming. They all mingled with our friends from the kink community—porn stars, academics, sex workers, and friends of the museum. It was a crazy cross-section of people. I brought Mahir as my date.

Although we always had opening-night parties, this one was especially rewarding. Typically, the various kink communities don't intersect. The pony play people don't hang out with the adult baby or balloon people and so on. But that night, everyone was together, proudly donning the clothes that reflected their various kinks. Everyone felt comfortable and exhilarated by the exhibition; there was a palpable buzz in the air.

Mahir and I stood in the exhibition room, a hot-pink gallery that encouraged patrons to touch and experiment with the artifacts of kink, such as a leather riding crop, a bondage hood, and an assortment of restraining devices. We designed it to be playful and bubbly—to counter the idea that kink is dark and foreboding—and it was. *Kink* was a candyland of sexual fantasy.

It would have been easy for Mahir to feel overwhelmed by his surroundings. I half-expected he would be. I needn't have worried. He approached it all with an energy and openness that I found very attractive. Mahir seemed to really be enjoying himself. He liked my coworkers and appeared to be proud of my work on the exhibition. With the success of *Kink,* and the way things were developing with Mahir, I allowed myself to feel encouraged—optimistic, even.

That's when he told me about his parents' visit.

"They're coming from Jordan for a month."

"Great!" I said. "I can't wait to meet them."

One look from him was all it took.

He continued. "It's really not a good idea for you to stop by the apartment when they're here. You understand, right?"

My friends had been right: the relationship would never amount to anything.

I could have pretended that I was surprised, but we both knew that I wasn't. And although I could have chalked it up to the religious divide, I knew it was something more.

In the months since Nick and I broke up, all the nights being a party girl, meeting men who made me feel like working as a curator of sex was the same thing as selling it, I'd inadvertently been sending Mahir the wrong messages. Heartbreak does funny things to people, I guess. And at the age of twenty-four, instead of putting out the signal that I was ready for another serious, committed relationship, I was doing the exact opposite. The museum wasn't just the place I worked; it didn't just shape the way I saw the world. It had become my identity. I had become "Sarah Sex," and it wasn't doing me any favors.

ten

Sex by Design

It was becoming hard to tell if I was the one obsessed with sex—from an academic perspective, of course—or if my particular career was a magnet for men who were. Or maybe the job really was changing me. After all, sex had become the center of my solar system. I was seeing sex in everything. It made sense, I guess. Our professions can inform the lens through which we see the world, and I was seeing everything through the lens of sex. Where once I saw a sea of businessmen, I now saw married men spending their time online searching for both women and men to have affairs with. (Although my e-mail can be found compromised in the Ashley Madison hack, I'm one of the few who can legitimately claim it was for professional purposes.) Where before a bruised ankle would signal nothing more than a clumsy encounter with a desk, I now wondered if it had been the result of ropes tied just a little too tightly. I was beginning to think that everyone, in his or her own particular, incredible, and creative way, was a sexual freak. Although an amazing revelation from an anthropological perspective, this realization was incompatible with the traditional happily-ever-after I coveted when I first began working at the museum. I was becoming cynical, if not straight-up disillusioned, with men in New York. That's where fate intervened—in a bar, of course.

Far from the glitz of the Meatpacking District, it was a generic sports bar with requisite wall-to-wall TV screens. It was a local spot, a block or two away from my apartment, and I hadn't even bothered to dress up. On a normal night out I would have felt naked without heels, makeup, and a blow-out. But that night, a freezing Tuesday, it wasn't about the scene. I would be drinking to support a good cause, raising money to teach inner city kids the sport of rugby. I called Jill and, capitalizing on her semester abroad in Scotland, dragged her out to be my wing woman for the evening.

I pulled my hair up into a messy bun and swaddled my body in a thick black sweater dress with a high collar. But even though I was going for incognito that night, I caught the eye of a tall, handsome blond guy.

"Can you sing?" he asked. "Can you raise your left eyebrow?" He had a cute Irish accent. Clearly, I was a magnet for foreign guys. But tonight I wasn't in the mood to be bothered, and that opening line totally set me off.

I threw my arm over Jill's shoulder and said, "I appreciate the effort but you're wasting your time. She's the only blonde in my life."

Jill looked at me, surprised. She'd seen countless guys chat me up and would usually roll her eyes when I humored random sketch-balls, especially the ones who were way too excited when they learned where I worked. But she wasn't amused with this blow-off.

Jill is one of the most grounded people in my world, so if she raises her eyebrows, I know I've made a misstep. Why had I responded so negatively to the guy? Maybe a part of me was still missing Nick. Maybe I was jaded after the way things ended with Mahir. Or maybe, and most likely, having sex dominate my life day after day, I had come to believe that every man was single-minded and sex obsessed. This was certainly what most of them showed me once they heard about my job. I'd automatically lumped this Irish fellow in with all the overeager men at bars who thought, after learning about my job, that I'd happily jump into their beds. But this poor guy didn't even know about the museum. Jill was right; I should apologize.

But the tall Irish guy with the funny questions was nowhere to be found.

"He was really cute," Jill said.

"Was he?" I said, looking around the bar to see if I could spot him. He was tall enough that he would stand out in the crowd. The fact that I didn't see him made it clear he'd left.

"What was that all about?"

"I don't know," I said. "I guess I thought he was just like all the other players in bars."

She shook her head. "You know, not everyone is just looking to get into your pants. Some guys might be worth the benefit of the doubt."

"Maybe," I said sheepishly. And I had a feeling she was right.

Then, to my surprise—and yes, delight—there he was again, grinning confidently as he walked back into the bar. Right up to me again.

Caught off guard, I scrambled to think of something to say. But he spoke first.

"My friend bet me I could never recover from your dismissal," he said, grinning. A bet between friends over a woman would normally have annoyed me, but I saw this as an opportunity to redeem myself.

I think we were both surprised at how readily I recited those ten digits. He clicked them carefully into his phone, told me his name was Jason, and said good-bye as Jill looked on approvingly.

It was a few nights later, when I was at a friend's birthday dinner at Ideya, a Latin American restaurant in Soho, that Jason texted me. Quite by chance, he was at Naked Lunch, a bar a few blocks away.

"Why don't you swing by here when you're done?" he said.

"Okay," I said. "But I'm bringing some friends."

We arrived as a big group, many of us chatting in Spanish. I bounded to the DJ booth to request the birthday girl's favorite Reggaeton song. It was only then, as we started dancing, that I saw Jason, with his mostly preppy all-American group looking on. It was as if we were a spectacle they had never seen before, a big departure from their jumping up and down to House of Pain.

A little over an hour into the night, my friends wanted to move on. Jason leaned over and kissed me good-bye. It was our first kiss. It wasn't a long kiss, but it caught me off guard. Just a simple honest kiss, and not a whiff of anything more. No request to go home with him. I must have looked confused.

"Don't forget," he said. "I'm just a nice Irish Catholic boy from Dublin." And with that he winked at me.

This was different from most of the guys I was meeting. I hoped I would see him again. But who really knew?

And besides—he had no clue what I did for a living.

→◆ ◆←

Exhibitions, like relationships, were opportunities to immerse myself in something new. And just like relationships, exhibitions are a lot of hard work.

With *Kink* officially launched, it was time to start planning the next exhibit: *Sex and Design/Design and Sex*. Three years into my tenure at MoSex, I found that talking about sex toys was almost second nature. I appreciated the array of historic sex toys I'd been exposed to, such as carved ivory dildos (even strap-ons) from the 1700s as well as my personal favorite, a box of "laughter devices," or *warai do-gu,* from early-twentieth-century Japan. This bento box of sex contained dildos, cock rings, and a wide range of sexual "accessories," skillfully handcrafted from buffalo horn, tortoiseshell, and wood. MoSex's own vibrator collection dates back to 1911, but in fact the earliest mechanical vibrator—a steam-powered contraption, the Manipulator, that took up a whole room—was invented by Dr. George Taylor in 1869. As cumbersome and perhaps comical as some of these items are, they serve as a tangible reminder that the pursuit of pleasure is timeless. Nevertheless, instead of looking toward the past, as so many of our exhibitions had, I was interested in capturing something in the current sexual zeitgeist: a revolution quietly taking place in the sex industry, one that was producing high-end luxury sex toys that were as technologically inspired as they were beautiful.

One of the museum's previous exhibitions, *Sex Machines: Photographs and Interviews* by Timothy Archibald had been my indoctrination, my first introduction to the world of sex inventors.

The first sex inventor I met was Alan Stein, creator of the ThrillHammer, an antique dentist chair wired to reach vibration speeds of up to 6500 rpm and rotation speeds of 150 rpm. Before joining the museum's collection, the ThrillHammer toured the United States, including a stop at the Chicken Ranch, one of the famous legal prostitution houses in Nevada. It was test-driven by many, many women on its way.

It's not just a glorified sex chair. The ThrillHammer allows the movements and speed of the machine to be controlled remotely by another person. It is an incredible early example of teledildonics, loosely defined as the integration of computer-controlled technology with the goal of helping achieve sexual stimulation and orgasm. There's a camera and monitor attached to a mechanical tentacle that wraps around the machine like an arm. Video footage of the user's full body streams so the machine can be controlled remotely, from the next room or across the world. In my first year working at the museum, we had teamed up with Dorkbot for a tech showcase event in which a live model engaged with the machine while footage was streamed from New York to a huge tech conference in San Francisco. Journalist Violet Blue was behind the ThrillHammer's controls in San Francisco.

After working on the sex machine exhibition, I couldn't read about emerging technologies, video games, or even 3D and HD televisions (for the record, some body parts are not best seen in such close detail) without thinking about a sexual application. When Nintendo's Wii came out in 2006, I knew it would be just a matter of time until people were standing in their living rooms simulating various acts, just as I'm certain that a whole world of sexual creativity will be unleashed as 3D printing becomes more widespread. People are already attempting to use 3D technology to print actual functioning penises.

If you buy into the premise of the movie *Her,* love affairs with our computer operating systems will become commonplace, and soon. Some believe that by 2050 robot brothels will be an industry standard.

With *Sex and Design,* I would explore how scientific innovations and high-end, luxury design were being applied to sex toys. Materials like Pyrex, surgical steel, wood, and even kinetic energy are revolutionizing this industry. This good news was in contrast to the bad: that many commercially available sex toys are made with phthalates, the chemical that gives plastic that recognizable smell—also a dangerous carcinogen. Companies get away with selling these toxic items by simply attaching the word *novelty,* implying that it shouldn't actually be used. And these dangerous chemicals aren't just found in specialty shops; many drugstore lubricants are full of unsavory additions like parabens, glycerin, hormones, silicones, and petroleum. For the first time, my exhibition research was changing the choices I made.

But the application of new materials is nothing new. As with our desire to capture sex with the latest recording technology— photography and film—we also have a history of applying new materials to a wide variety of other sexually related objects. Condoms were once made of animal intestines, then rubber (originally meant to be reused), and later latex. It makes me, for one, thankful for sexual innovation.

Some new technologies are even serving a larger social good, like nanotechnology used in the production of next-generation condoms. Through the process of electrospinning, a new nanometer-size fiber is being studied for its ability to prevent pregnancy and the transmission of sexually transmitted infections. At-home HIV tests, male birth control pills, and bras that detect breast cancer are all in development

Now, a whole new wave of technology is improving sex devices—making them safer, more pleasurable, and increasingly personalized to our tastes, desires, and ideologies. The green movement, in particular, is making inroads into the world of sex. Because latex condoms are treated with a milk-based enzyme, the condom manufacturer Glyde stepped in to provide a vegan-friendly alternative.

→◆ ◆←

Through the world of sex design and invention I met a host of talented designers: Ethan Imogen, who founded the popular sex toy line Jimmyjane; conceptual designer Shiri Zinn, whose pretty pink Minx vibrator is a variable-speed sex toy set with Swarovski crystals and a feather tail; and Betony Vernon, who, according to British *GQ,* is "the haute jewelry designer whose 'sado-chic' brings an aesthete's eye to S&M accessories." I also had the pleasure of meeting Rhett Butler (yes, that's his real name), who created a line of butt plugs and other high-end sex toys for Kiki de Montparnasse.

Rhett has his own housewares design shop in Soho, which is how he ended up wandering into Kiki one day. Inspired by the application of high-end design toward sex, Rhett approached Kiki about a collaboration. Always thinking creatively about new materials, Rhett found an incredible filament that was used in military parachutes to produce a string of pearls that could do double duty as a necklace and a bondage instrument. Similarly, he created a locket that turns into a vibrator. He launched a genre of luxury items that had secret sexual functions. Personally, I was a fan; I loved that if I wore one of his creations, no one would be the wiser. Still, I had no illusions that Jason would ever give me a vibrating locket for Valentine's Day.

Rhett's innovations were in good company with artist-entrepreneurs like Matt McMullen. Matt's company, Abyss Creations, invented the RealDoll. For many, the RealDoll is not just the ultimate sex toy; it's an integral part of a sexual lifestyle. The RealDoll has a fully articulated skeleton and fully customizable parts. You can choose everything from breast size down to the details of pubic-hair styling, makeup, and nail color. These dolls are a remarkable approximation of a real person. Within the museum, the information label next to the RealDoll reads:

Female RealDoll 2 Body A

ReadDoll 2 Face M "Brooklyn"

Medium Skin Tone, French Manicure Nails

Shaved Pubic Hair

Courtesy of Abyss Creations

Consumers customize their RealDoll 2 by choosing from several different body types, face shapes, and many other grooming details. Able to be penetrated vaginally, anally, and orally, RealDolls can withstand up to 400 lbs of weight and are designed to simulate the experience of having sex with an actual person.

The dolls can cost up to ten thousand dollars—worth every penny for the owners who have complete sexual and emotional relationships with these creations. The RealDoll is made from an extraordinarily high-grade silicone—yet another example of the way human sexuality benefits from technology.

And on the subject of dolls, artist Michael Sullivan transforms Barbie dolls and GI Joes into sex-crazed robots to star in his animated film, *The Sex Lives of Robots*. Mike is a petite man with long white hair who wears snug seventies-era T-shirts with rainbow suspenders. His pant pockets are perpetually weighed down with doll parts and the tools he uses as a prop maker. As with many artists, his motivation wasn't necessarily to finish a project, but to explore its creative angles to the fullest. He has continued to work on his short film for years and years, contemplating the nuances of how robots would reproduce. I imagine it to be a grand sexual opus in waiting.

I was encountering high-end latex designers such as Demask, based in Amsterdam. When their Torpedo Tit Catsuit arrived for the *Kink* exhibition, just my size, it was so beautifully crafted I had to try it on. And in another cross between sex and fashion, I was also fortunate enough to meet the perfumers commissioned by Lady Gaga to create a fragrance with scent notes of semen. (For the record: anytime someone smells this particular note without knowing its origin, they either pull away repulsed or they grab their throat, knowing that it is somehow familiar to them, but just not able to put their finger on how.)

Just as the artifacts of sex collectors informed my understanding of the past, these artisans of sex—real-life, sexually inspired Willy Wonkas—educated me on where sex was heading in the future. RingU, for example, is a ring worn by long-distance lovers that can produce the sensation of various types of hugs through Bluetooth technology (a Mini-Hug is a short squeeze, an Intense Hug is a long squeeze, and an Urgent Hug is expressed in a series of squeezes). Oh MY BOD is a sex toy that hooks up to an iPod, vibrating to the pulse of music (not surprisingly connecting with a loyal DJ and club scene following) that can be controlled remotely by a lover halfway around the world.

Created only a few years ago, many of the objects featured in the *Sex and Design/Design and Sex* exhibition are almost dinosaurs in the fast-paced world of sex technology. Today, virtual reality and artificial intelligence are the new terrain for these technological pioneers.

→◆ ◆←

From Mike's robots to Matt's RealDolls to butt plugs made of jade and vibrators encrusted with diamonds, a new crop of designers, inventors, and entrepreneurs is bringing luxury, pleasure, and ergonomic design to new levels. These innovators are "sex workers" just like me, and through them I was finding my own community of people. (I very purposely use the phrase *sex worker,* since I think society often doesn't distinguish between those who work with sex and those who engage in sexual activities as their profession.) I was learning there were others like me. Those who had "mainstream" lives, but happened to make their livelihood through the sex industry—without actually having sex with anyone in the process. When I met with these people, I didn't have to explain what I did. I didn't have to legitimize my job. With these people, there was no introductory hurdle. They understood that I was just a regular person with an extraordinary job.

Unfortunately, that understanding did not always translate

elsewhere. One of our ads for the exhibition triggered what I liked to call "the nipple police."

Many a magazine editor has called the museum, alarmed when they believe they see a nipple or penis in one of our advertisements. (I am certain our ads are reviewed with a microscope.) Maybe it's their eyes playing tricks on them or a desire to see something titillating, but we often have to remind them that a shadow may in fact be just a shadow. Even with far racier ads out there, the word "sex" in our title is a red flag to bullish censors.

One morning, I was pulled aside by our director of marketing and PR. "So we have a little problem. Someone complained about the Lap Juicer. We're pulling the ad."

"What's wrong with it? Isn't it just a picture of the artifact, its name, and the name of the museum? What could possibly be wrong with that?"

"Apparently some woman was livid that her four-year-old daughter was exposed to a Lap Juicer."

Its name packs a punch, at least from an aesthetic perspective, but it was probably one of the most subtle items in our collection. You could easily find far more graphic images throughout the same newspaper.

The Lap Juicer was created for lap dancers: they place a half an orange on the juicer, and through the movements of their body, they force the juice out of the fruit. The juice is collected in a small glass and, at the end, it's handed to the viewer. Although a fascinating concept, the average adult would have no idea of the object's use without a detailed explanation. I had watched thousands of patrons stand in front of its case, tilting their heads, clearly wondering, "What the hell are you meant to do with that?" It seemed pretty unlikely that this four-year-old was able to figure out its intended use from one glance at her mother's morning newspaper. It was clearly just the concept behind the piece that the woman found offensive.

In the end, *Sex and Design* coincided with a period when the hidden objects of our sex lives became mainstream. If I had mentioned Jimmyjane just before the exhibition launched, very few people would have known what I was talking about. Only a couple of celebrities were buying them. Now a huge number of my girlfriends know about these products. *Sex and Design* hit right at a time when my world and the mainstream began to converge, and the exhibition captured this moment beautifully.

I was settling in to my unconventional role at the museum, starting to feel more comfortable with giant dildos and sex machines, and finding my footing and my tribe in the process. I only hoped Jason could become comfortable with it, too.

eleven

Down the Rabbit Hole

In the beginning, we talked about our jobs.

An Irish citizen, Jason had lived and worked in every corner of the globe. He had recently moved to New York from LA, where he had been working with the studios. With his Hollywood stories (Jason lived, in his own words, "like a poor man's *Entourage*"), he struck me as a privileged playboy. And he was older than me, too—thirty-three years to my twenty-four.

I felt like we came from two different worlds.

Jason was a management consultant, and the stories of his workdays seemed so grown-up and professional. My contributions were more, let's just say . . . intimate.

"What you put up your butt really does matter," I told him. This little gem was my latest takeaway thought from the *Sex and Design* exhibition—the importance of using sex toys that were made from nontoxic materials.

He seemed less than dazzled by this revelation.

I continued to lob sexual trivia his way, like the fact that early sex dolls used by sailors were known as "dames de voyage." The oldest forms of dildos, I told him, were called "olisbos." I wasn't telling him this for shock value; I truly found everything I was learning fascinating. It meant something to me that sex objects were becoming so beautiful and luxurious that designer coffee table books were being made on the topic. It felt like a validation of my field and my career choice.

But Jason wasn't impressed with my treasure trove of sexual insights, and I wasn't impressed that he kept taking me to the trendiest restaurants.

I didn't know it at the time, but Jason wasn't the type of guy to take a woman out for a fancy Saturday night dinner date. He looked like that guy—he was generous and elegant, always wearing a suit—but in reality, he had learned that it was better to grab a casual drink or an informal coffee than be locked in to a long, expensive night with someone who may not be a good match. If only I had known that he was trying to impress me because he thought I was special.

Our first "official" date was at La Esquina. On the ground level, La Esquina looks like a run-down taco stand, but then you notice a person with a clipboard. If your name is on the list, a magical door opens and you'll walk downstairs into what seems like a basement. The next thing you know you're walking through a working kitchen. Around the bend, you're greeted in a cavern filled with dripping candles, a DJ spinning in the corner, and—when we were there—some of the most beautiful people in New York. At five seven, I was the shortest woman in the room, by far.

In 2007, La Esquina was impossible to get into; Jason had to do a lot of maneuvering to get the prime-time reservation. I wish

I had understood the significant efforts he was making at the time, and that this sort of first date was as rare for Jason as it was for me. Instead, it was the first of many misunderstandings between us: who we were, how we operated, what we wanted. We both played our cards close to the vest, and it would take a lot of work to overcome that.

The more showy Jason was, the more I thought he was just a player. And the more I talked about sex, the more he thought I was a woman who wasn't interested in a relationship, but just wanted to have a good time. Still, we both must have known, on some level, that something deeper was going on, because we continued to see each other. In Jason I recognized someone who had the same appetite for life and nocturnal mischief that I did, someone who wanted to turn life into an adventure. Sharp-witted, he challenged me and asked me questions. He made me think a little deeper about my assertions. And because he was so different from anyone I'd ever met before, or have since, he was genuinely exciting to be around. So I put up with the pretentious restaurants, and he put up with my unconventional dinner conversation.

One night we were on our way to a movie in Times Square. The only dinner we had time for was a quick stop at McDonald's on the way.

I told him it was the sweetest date we'd had.

Soon after that, still in the getting-to-know-you stage, Jason had wanted to make a gesture toward my Mexican heritage. "I found a really well reviewed authentic spot for dinner," he told me excitedly. He texted me the address of "a cute little Mexican place" and told me to meet him there after work. I was always excited to see Jason, but I was especially touched by this effort to connect with my heritage. When I got to the street, however, I couldn't find the restaurant, despite walking up and down the block three times. I checked the address in my phone, but the only restaurant, aside from an Irish pub, was a Chipotle. And then it hit me: this guy had never heard of Chipotle.

I think that's when I started to fall just a little bit in love with him.

→◆ ◆←

"Sarah, get ready to pack your bags," Dan said, bounding into the museum one morning. Because of the open-office layout, there was no hiding from his unpredictable bursts of inspiration.

"Um, okay?" I said.

He dropped a printout of a magazine article on my desk and waited expectantly while I skimmed the first page. The piece, from *Seed* magazine, was titled "Against Nature?" It was about a museum exhibition that explored various same-sex relationships in the animal kingdom, an unprecedented exhibition based on research found in a book called *Biological Exuberance: Animal Homosexuality and Natural Diversity* by Bruce Bagemihl. The eight-hundred-page encyclopedia, which details more than five hundred species that engage in same-sex relationships, was not new at that point, but the science was still groundbreaking.

"Interesting," I said. Then I saw that the museum was in Oslo, Norway. Even more interesting.

"I need you to go next week. Check it out. See if this is something that would translate for our audience."

I'd never been to Norway. I loved to travel. The museum was paying. It was win-win.

The only thing that was better than a free trip was a free trip with a friend. But who would be up for a last-minute jaunt to

Europe? The first person I thought of was my friend Diana from college. She was spontaneous and, at the moment, between jobs. I had barely finished my pitch when she agreed to go.

As always, the museum was tight with money, so my travel budget was rather limited. I found an inexpensive hotel room that had space for a bed and little else, but that didn't really matter because, thanks to Diana's planning skills, we had a full sightseeing agenda. We really only needed the hotel to sleep and shower.

We were off and running the minute our plane landed in Oslo. And we threw ourselves into Norwegian culture: fresh fish, booze, and very late, very cold winter nights. As the only brunettes in the crowded bars, we stood out as exotic visitors. Diana and I always spoke Spanish when we were together, a leftover tradition from our college days, one that only seemed to increase our foreign allure. We got plenty of attention from the cute Norwegian guys, but Jason was on my mind. I took that as a good sign.

I woke up that first morning suffering from both jet lag and a hangover, but there was no time to indulge my exhaustion because my contacts at the Natural History Museum wanted to meet bright and early. And so I trudged up the hill through steady snowfall and bone-chilling cold to meet with the curators.

The museum was a magnificent stone building surrounded by acres of land. It looked like a manor house out of a PBS period drama. I was met by a welcoming group who—after a round of introductions—led me through the exhibition.

My goal was to see if the material at *Against Nature* would work at the Museum of Sex. It's one thing to read about an exhibition, but the in-person experience is often much different. Such was the case with the Oslo exhibition.

Upon entering the exhibition hall, I was immediately confronted with a zoo of taxidermies, arranged in Kama Sutra positions that must have left the taxidermist either highly amused or completely appalled. One curious installation featured a colony of penguins, several of which were accented with pink scarves, which was meant to be a visual representation of the portion of the species that engages in same-sex relationships.

What struck me most wasn't the penguins. And it wasn't the pink scarves. (Which, frankly, struck me as clichéd, if not offensive.) It was the fact that I was viewing this particular exhibition alongside a large group of kindergartners.

In the United States, sex education for teens and young adults is a deeply political and polarizing issue. Not in Norway, where kindergartners are taught about the diversity of animal sexuality. How different from the United States, where the Museum of Sex was off limits to those below eighteen years of age. In our early years, MoSex was unable to advertise in the subway (that has since changed), and tour bus guides traveling down Fifth Avenue were reprimanded for even pointing out the museum. I was definitely in culture shock. Yes, college professors regularly sent their students to the Museum of Sex, but even this pushed boundaries. In my opinion, many of our exhibitions were appropriate and educational for older teens, but I'd long ago accepted that this was a battle I would not win, and probably was not mine to fight.

And so, surrounded by children at a "gay" animal sex exhibition (I use this for emphasis, but really this is a descriptor used for human categories of sexual orientation and we have no idea if animals identify as such), I knew the Museum of Sex would need to make a lot of changes for an adult American audience. It wasn't that we didn't want to show same-sex activity in the animal kingdom—it's just that we would have to show it amid the wider range of sexual activity. After all, we were the Museum of Sex. If we were going to explore animal sexuality, we needed to go all the way. I just had to figure out how.

Gazing at my new friends, the pink-scarved penguins, my jet lag disappeared to be replaced by a feeling of exhilaration I was starting to recognize as growing passion for my work. That was the moment I knew that the next year of my life would be dedicated to learning everything I could about animal sex.

As a parting gift, the museum curators gave me a copy of Bagemihl's weighty *Biological Exuberance*. Poor Diana spent the eight-hour plane ride back to New York listening to my excitement as I Post-it-noted pages and scrawled my thoughts onto a yellow legal pad. Good friend that she is, Diana just grinned, encouraging my sexually inspired nerd-out.

But halfway through the flight, my fatigue—and reality—caught up to me.

"This is going to be intense. To do this right, this project will take over my life." It would be an immense amount of work, and I just knew that I would be immersed in research around the clock. I hated to admit it, but I was also thinking about Jason. I wondered if, in the near future, I might be factoring a relationship more into my life.

"You're already halfway down the rabbit hole," Diana said. "And who knows what those kinky rabbits are doing down there."

twelve

Mating in the Wild

At most natural history museums, it's rare for an animal's penis to be shown. I have earnestly looked. In this "new natural history," I wanted to present an uncensored story of the natural world, taking our understanding of animal sexuality beyond the confines of reproduction and mating and toward orientation and cognition. I felt that by exploring sex, the most intimate part of life, where it is often said humans are most "animal-like," visitors to MoSex could appreciate the significance of research on animal sexuality and, perhaps, extrapolate, applying these concepts to larger issues regarding human sexuality. Maybe there was more than one way to look at Darwinism.

But first, I needed to deal with human sexuality on a much smaller scale: my own.

What was this "thing" happening between me and Jason?

When we met for dinner the night after I returned home, it struck me that the time apart had somehow crystallized what I felt for him. It was as if the relationship had matured months in just the short time we'd been apart. And I was clearly not alone in my feelings, because halfway through dinner, Jason said, "If I still know you in May, would you like to come to a wedding with me in Italy?"

I swallowed hard and tried my best to act nonchalant.

"If I still know you—and if I still like you—that sounds like fun."

He also seemed, for the first time, genuinely interested in my work. Science was apparently sexier to him than sex toys. He listened intently about my trip, and when I shared my vision for the Museum of Sex's version of *The Sex Lives of Animals* exhibition, he said, "This sounds like it could be really valuable from an educational standpoint."

"You think so?" I said, more thrilled by his praise than I wanted to admit.

"Absolutely," he said. And then, with a smile, "But what kind of 'sex collector' can you call for this sort of thing?"

He was joking. But he had hit on something that I was already grappling with. This exhibition would be steeped in science in a way that nothing else I'd worked on had been. It was leaps and bounds beyond *Sex and Design* or *Sex and the Moving Image*. Yes, *Kink* relied on psychology and the science of human sexuality, but nothing like what I would be confronted with in this new project. I needed a guide.

→◆ ◆←

Joan Roughgarden is professor emerita at Stanford and is the author of *Evolution's Rainbow: Diversity, Gender, and Sexuality in Nature and People*. She was mentioned in the original article about the Oslo museum, and I knew she was the very person I needed to guide me through this intricate research project. I was thrilled when she agreed to join the team and serve as the exhibition's primary content advisor.

A rock star of the scientific world, Joan's controversial critique of Darwin's sexual selection theory made her work politically charged. Whereas Darwin positioned sex and partner selection in the natural world as an extension of the drive to reproduce, Joan's work looked at the scientific research compiled in the more than 150 years since Darwin's assertions and posited: maybe evolution isn't just driven by heterosexual behavior and reproduction. Could it be possible, for example, that the male peacock's brilliant feathers didn't exist solely to attract a female peacock? A huge simplification, of course, but maybe they were just as enticing to other male peacocks.

Writing in a different era, Darwin failed to discuss why the male peacock sometimes seemed disinterested in the females and were instead attracted to the bright plumage of a fellow male. Joan's work forces us to address the notion that not all animal relationships are heterosexual and reproductive, a major chink in the armor of Darwinian sexual selection theory.

Joan's groundbreaking ideas challenged the status quo in the scientific community—and made her a target. Her work alone would have made this the case, but a sex reassignment operation in 1998, in which she shifted her identity from Jonathan to Joan, likely compounded the uproar. Though Joan and I never discussed this aspect of her life (one's gender identity has no bearing on one's professional credentials), undeterred she kept researching, publishing, and teaching. I can only assume that she must have known the Pandora's box she was opening in putting her research out into the universe, and while some might not have been so brave, this act has broadened the thinking of many people.

Under Joan's direction, I assembled a team of twelve acclaimed scientists, evolutionary biologists, primatologists, and others to bring little-known research to the public. With their expertise, I began to create an exhibition that I hoped would challenge our preconceived ideas about what is "natural"—a word often invoked to help us make sense of our world—and counter some of the incorrect "natural facts" we have long taken as truth.

I started with the list of misconceptions Joan counters throughout her work:

- An organism is solely male or female for life.
- Males are bigger and stronger than females, on average.
- Females, not males, give birth.
- Only two genders exist, corresponding to the two sexes.
- Males and females look different from each other.
- The male has the penis and the female lactates.
- Males control females.
- Females prefer monogamy and males want multiple partners.

In every one of these cases, it turns out what most of us believe as true is completely false.

I was quickly overwhelmed by how misinformed we are about what is actually happening in the natural world—and how our misconceptions have led to flawed social structures on a grand scale. How could we be so wrong, so often? And, more important, could we start thinking differently?

Fully immersed in exhibition planning, I left work excited

every day, wanting to share all the crazy new things I had learned. In stark contrast to his initial attitude about my work, Jason embraced my childlike excitement for my new favorite topic: the sex lives of animals. Finally warming to my unusual career, he listened intently as I rattled off a long list of penis facts.

Did you know barnacles have penises forty times the length of their bodies? Being sedentary, this length is necessary to get to their barnacle partner. Evolution at work.

Or that the blue whale has the longest penis, nearly eight feet long? Yet nature isn't always that generous: the silverback gorilla's penis, on average, measures only 1.25 inches.

Or that some animals have a "cloaca," an orifice that serves both a sexual function as well as an excretory one.

Believe it or not, the greatest penis diversity exists within the insect world. Insects often have barbs and spikes decorating their shafts, used to anchor the male within the female. Some animals even have an actual penis bone, also known as a baculum or os penis. Penis bones, found in some mammals, support the erection of an animal during copulation. They come in various shapes and sizes based on the particular animal species and can serve as a tool in differentiating similar species. (No, humans do not possess penis bones, even though the word "boner" would make you think they do.) Although lacking penis bones, snakes and lizards evolved to have two penises. Called a hemipenis, this two-pronged V-shaped penis allows mating from either the right or left side, alternating for each copulation.

Day by day my list of penis facts grew. I soon learned banana slugs have penises on their heads and that copulation is commonly followed by apophallation, or chewing off the penis by a partner. If you're cringing, get ready for this: banana slugs have even been known to auto-apophallate—chew off their *own* penis. And it does not regenerate. Flatworms are even more aggressive, practicing a form of "penis fencing." As a hermaphroditic species, meaning it possesses the reproductive organs of both the male and female, each flatworm has a sharp penis that it wields as a weapon to determine which flatworm will be inseminated. The battle ends when one successfully pierces the skin of the other and ejaculates. The inseminated partner assumes the female role and carries the fertilized eggs.

Then there's the Argentine lake duck with its corkscrew-shaped penis measuring at seventeen and a half inches and the reciprocal female's corkscrew-shaped vagina.

The variations are seemingly endless, and this diversity in the size, shape, and color of genitals is useful in taxonomy—the study of classification of animals, objects, and ideas—helping us to identify species. Genitalia can serve as signaling structures— signs of arousal or fertility to a species' potential mates. These cues might include changing the color of genitalia and/or the release of perfumes and other biologically arousing odors.

Surprisingly, genitalia are not always the best criteria in differentiating males from females of the same species. For instance, male and female whales look almost identical externally, as the penis is protected by the genital slit when not being used, and the testes remain in the body cavity instead of descending. In some primate species, such as the woolly monkey, spider monkey, and galago (also known as the bush baby, these nocturnal primates are typically smaller than a pound), the clitoris of females is the same size or larger than the male penis. In the spotted hyena, females have a full replica of the male external genital structure. Not only do female spotted hyenas urinate through this penis-like appendage, they also give birth through it.

You don't have to be exposed to this material for long before it becomes apparent that the idea of "right" or "normal" does not exist in nature. There's no "normal" shape for a penis or vulva, no "right" way to copulate, and few, if any, structures show more variation than the genitals. But in the case of polar bears, environmental issues are accelerating this variation.

Polar bears are at the top of the fatty-food marine chain, meaning they consume a tremendous amount of fish per day. But as environmental pollutants fill our waters and invade the food chain, the polar bear's food source becomes contaminated as well. High levels of pollutants such as polychlorinated biphenyls (PCBs) and dichlorodiphenyltrichloroethane (DDTs) are absorbed into their bodies through the fish they eat, causing an alarming physical change. The penises of male polar bears are shrinking, and the clitorises of female polar bears are growing.

Back in 1996, while doing fieldwork in the Arctic, Professors Andrew Derocher and Øystein Wiig began noticing that the clitoris of the polar bears they had been tracking were enlarged. Ten years after that, Christian Sonne discovered that chemicals such as PCBs and DDTs were being transported by sea currents and air systems from the industrial world into this region just east of Greenland. The penises of East Greenland polar bears were shrinking. At this rate, it is unknown if the two sexes will be able to copulate effectively if the pollution continues. So not only are the ecosystems of polar bears disappearing because of global warming, but these same environmental contaminants are endangering the procreation of the species.

If there was ever a fact that could raise environmental aware-ness, I believe it would be this: Guys, if you don't protect the en-vironment, your penis could shrink.

In bed one night, I told Jason, "The vervet monkey, native to the southeast of Africa, has a bright-blue, almost turquoise scrotum. As the rank of a male vervet rises and falls, the inten-sity of the blue changes."

He looked at me and smiled.

"Sarah, no matter how much scientific research you have to back you up, you'll never convince me that blue balls is a good thing."

thirteen

The Girl in the Red Dress

May arrived so quickly I hadn't had time to second-guess my decision to go with Jason to the wedding in Italy—a trip that required a pit stop in Ireland to meet his parents. Jason had downplayed this when he'd asked me to join: "It's no big deal. Separate bedrooms, just a quick hello, and, besides, haven't you always wanted to see Dublin? It's a great city!" It did sound great. But I didn't quite know what to expect. Would Jason introduce me as his girlfriend? Did he regularly bring women "home" to Ireland, or was this significant? And if he did bring women home, somehow I doubted any of them had jobs in the sex field. I couldn't help but worry that my career would clash with the conservative, pedigreed family I was about to meet.

As my relationship was maturing into the next stage, so was the museum.

That month, May 2007, we were hosting our first gala. With a serious, scientific exhibition in the works, and a major fund-raiser on the calendar, the museum was finally becoming less of a curiosity and more of a genuine, New York institution. A woman named Noelle was in charge of the affair. She'd been at the museum about a year, but as always, since the staff was so small, we all pitched in. I helped stuff envelopes for the invitations and gave some input about the setup, but I was otherwise fully consumed with planning the exhibit—which is why I didn't realize that Jason booked our flight to Dublin on the same night as the gala. By the time I grasped what I had done, it was too late to change our plans.

I didn't have time to worry about this scheduling snafu, though. *The Sex Lives of Animals* was consuming most of my waking thoughts, including the interesting notion that many of these animals had better sex lives than most of us humans.

This certainly seemed true for bonobos, our closest genetic relatives. Bonobos, once known as pygmy chimpanzees, have sex *constantly*. They have sex in male-male, female-female, and intergenerational relationships. They have sex to encourage sharing and cooperation, they have sex to ease social tensions, and they have sex for pleasure. Sex is the "language" of their culture. Although they do not have a verbal language, they do have a highly developed sign language that they use during sex. So they can communicate things like "turn around," "bend over," "open your legs," and other keys phrases to enhance the moment. As a matriarchal society, the bonobo's most common sexual act is called G-G rubbing, or genito-to-genito rubbing, which occurs between two females. Since the female bonobo clitoris is nearly two and a half inches long, penetration can actually occur during bouts of G-G rubbing. Bonobos have also been known to exchange treats such as sugarcane for sex, like a gift given during dating, or something more closely aligned to sex work in our parlance.

While working on the exhibition (and later, when reading glowing reviews on it) I realized part of the exhibition's appeal: animals make it safe to talk about sex. Somehow talking about orgasms, sex toys, and threesomes through the world of science, particularly through animals, opens people's minds and piques their curiosity. Science can distance sex from our human anxieties and fears, even if many of the acts discussed are the same. In my opinion, one of the greatest achievements of *The Sex Lives of Animals* is that it granted people permission to speak openly and ask questions about sex. Like insecure teenagers, few people want to raise their hands and admit they don't know something about sex, but in the land of animal sex, this burden is lifted. How many people know that banana slugs have a penis on top of their heads?

Immersing myself in the world of animal sex made me wonder if the constraints of our society, our hang-ups and misunderstandings, have made us "forget" how to follow our instincts when it comes to sex. Can we stop getting so stuck inside our own heads? Can we divorce our preconceived notions of sex long enough to figure out what truly turns us on? For instance, we've spent centuries demonizing masturbation, but one visit to the zoo will show you that animals don't really care who is watching as they do what comes naturally. The same goes for intercourse.

Although science warns us not to compare too directly between what occurs in the animal kingdom and within the human sphere, the naturalization of sex as a form of universal pleasure, rather than just a mechanism for reproduction, was a very important takeaway for those who visited the exhibition. If there was nothing unnatural about what animals were doing, whether it be masturbation, using sex toys (any found object—sticks, leaves, plant, gourds—can all be transformed into a tool of stimulation), engaging in group sex, same-sex relationships, or more advanced moves, like blowhole sex, why had humans made it all so complicated? Maybe this was the obstacle impeding our sexual satisfaction.

→◆ ◆←

The night of the gala, I dressed in a bright-red, form-fitting, one-shoulder dress and five-inch gold heels that made me close to six feet tall. I felt like I was in my very own fairy tale. With Jason by my side, I walked into the Angel Orensantz Center, a beautiful Gothic building originally constructed in 1849 as a synagogue. After years of decline and vandalism, the building was purchased in 1986 by Spanish artist Angel Orensantz, who converted it into a gallery and performance space. It's now a coveted destination for weddings and parties. Sarah Jessica Parker and Mathew Broderick even got married there.

Perez Hilton was the emcee, and our marquee performer was Dita Von Teese, the most famous burlesque star in the world. She was going to dazzle the crowd with her famous bathtub striptease. I'd seen her perform a month or two before at a club, where I stood just a few feet from Marilyn Manson, her husband at the time. She looked like a porcelain doll with the most perfect body you could imagine.

Dita's supplies were shipped to the venue ahead of time. Unfortunately, her golden bathtub arrived damaged—a fact we discovered only an hour before the performance. Frantic, Lizzie, our collections manager, and I ran around the Lower East Side looking for pieces of wood and glue to patch up the tub. In the midst of this insanity, Dita arrived. Thankfully, she was lovely. We got the tub fixed—and covered it with gold glitter—but the next challenge was getting the water temperature exactly right. Nothing in my anthropological studies had prepared me for this particular task. It wasn't that Dita was a diva. Far from it. The correct water temperature was vital to her performance: too hot or too cold, her fair skin would turn red and ruin the entire aesthetic. Like I said, her skin is flawless, and red blotches would ruin the visual perfection of her show. Luckily, her team took over, and I was able to relax and enjoy the party. Well, relax for a moment at least.

Dita's performance would be the highlight of the evening, but I didn't get to see it. Like Cinderella at the ball, I had a deadline. One hour into the party, Jason and I were battling New York City traffic in the rain on our dash to JFK.

We arrived at the airport with only minutes to spare. In a hurry, I began dividing up the contents of the gala's gift bag, which I had grabbed as we ran out the door. Vibrators and cock rings, lubricants and a sex game book—everything you would imagine in a Museum of Sex gift bag—I frantically shoved into my checked bag and hand luggage. I didn't have time to think about airport security. A big mistake.

While I stood next to the security station, the attendant slowly pulled out the nearly two dozen sex toys as I heard the last boarding call request on the loudspeaker.

My coach had officially turned into a pumpkin.

The agent turned the items over and over in her hands, trying to identify the mysterious objects that had set off the scanners.

Unlike typical novelty toys, many of these were skillfully designed to obscure their purpose. My collection confounded her.

"So . . . what are these?" she asked as she leaned in closely.

"Vibrators," I said quickly. There was no time to sugarcoat it.

With a look of disgust—perhaps imagining she had just handled recently used sex toys—the agent waved me onward. As I stuffed the loot back into my bag, I caught Jason staring from a few yards away with a look I couldn't quite decipher.

The important thing was that my sex toys and I were allowed to board the flight.

When we arrived in Dublin in the early morning hours, Jason's brother was waiting at the airport. Their excitement in seeing each other and eagerness to get back to the house left no time for me to find something more appropriate to wear. And so I arrived at the front gate of his refined family home—it even had a name, Hollypark House—still in my red dress and gold heels. Mortified, I kept my game face on as I sat with his parents for breakfast.

Jason told me ahead of time we would have separate bedrooms, and my first night in the house I realized that this was his idea—not his parents'. We may have spent the previous night at a party for the Museum of Sex, where I'd helped prep a burlesque star to get naked in a giant bathtub, but we were now in his childhood home, and I was experiencing a side of him that was surprisingly conservative.

Once we were in Tuscany, I saw yet another side to Jason. We were staying in an old castle with other members of the wedding party—all very *Four Weddings and a Funeral*. This was the first time I was meeting his best friends from childhood, and the first time I was really seeing him in his element. I realized quickly that Irish weddings are crazy, drunken affairs. Really wild.

Instead of ending at eleven as most American weddings do, the dancing and the drink go on until the next morning. Each of Jason's friends had their own well-practiced dance moves: flips, somersaults, and more than one "worm" across the stone dance floor. Even brides have been known to stage dive off the wedding's giant speakers, alongside her exuberant guests. And although I'd always thought of Jason as the loudest and craziest among his friends—the guy who needed to be the center of attention at a party—here among his oldest friends, he seemed one of the more reserved of the pack. What's more, four months into our relationship, he was treating me like a girlfriend, not just a date.

It was an important trip for us. Jason became more multidimensional to me. And I think that, being with me outside New York, seeing me away from my job and how I fit in with his family and friends, Jason was seeing me differently, too. I guess that attending a wedding can be a pivotal moment for a couple. And the stunning Tuscan location made it easy to get caught up in how romantic it all was. And it didn't hurt how strikingly handsome he was in a tux. For the first time, I started thinking about a future with this guy.

fourteen

F*cking Like Animals

For months following my trip to Dublin and Tuscany, I worked obsessively to turn a fascinating but complicated barrage of scientific information into a manageable exhibition. Although I gave a three-hundred-word limit to my stable of scientists, their submissions consistently ran pages long. I guess they were so excited to share their life's work that they forgot that museum text has to be accessible to a wide audience. Museum text should be informative, providing the "who, what, when, where, and why" patrons need in order to understand and appreciate a particular artifact. But it also has to be nuanced to help create that "sticky moment" we're always after. There's a real art to both writing and editing museum text. And of course it also has to be correct, which is why I shared all of my edited material with Joan Roughgarden, who ensured everything was scientifically accurate.

We were amassing quite a collection of photographs and

videos for the exhibition; still, we needed something three-dimensional to engage visitors. Unlike the museum in Oslo, we didn't want taxidermies, which are expensive and also very traditional—old-fashioned, even. We wanted something different. Our goal was to make a new natural history and move away from the approach that had reigned supreme for far too long. So I found a Norwegian artist named Rune Olsen, a talented sculptor who agreed to create scientifically rooted installations for us.

Every day brought new revelations: animals having sex for pleasure; species participating in group sex; animals masturbating; animals engaging in same-sex activity. If I was astonished— someone who at this point was nearly immune to shock—I can only imagine what the average museumgoer would think.

We were keen to dispel the monumental misconception that animal sexuality is tied solely to reproduction and to make the point that masturbation in the animal kingdom is far from rare. Male orangutans, for example, are resourceful enough to poke holes in leaves, insert their penises, and then pull the leaf back and forth to stimulate the shafts of their penises. I've seen videos of elephants humping giant yoga balls inside their enclosures, and a giant tortoise that found a particularly seductive set of steps in someone's backyard. Take a minute to look up "walrus masturbating" on YouTube. While you might not be able to hear it over the crowd's laughter at the zoo, the sound of a male walrus stroking his penis with his front flippers is referred to as a "strum call," similar to the sound produced by strumming the strings of a guitar. It's pretty clear that these animals aren't simply trying to procreate.

Obviously, animals can't articulate their experience of orgasms. But scientists have observed all of the same characteristics found in humans: increased heart rate, a quickening of breath, and excited vocalizations. Based on these parallels, many scientists conclude that sex is pretty enjoyable for animals, be it as part of a couple, alone, or even in a group. Yes, many animals are fans of group sex.

White-tailed deer are just one of several species that engage in group sex. Horseshoe crabs, sea hares, garter snakes, and slipper limpets participate in large configurations called "mating balls" and "mating chains." Snakes will form a giant ball or chain in which they are sequentially linked. Insects and many species of frogs also mate in groups.

Group animal sex can occur among multiple partners of the same sex or in mixed groups. Sometimes animals engage in group sex simply for pleasure, sometimes for reproductive benefits. It makes sense: if a large group has sex at the same time, then their young will be born at the same time, providing a better chance of survival against predators.

Spinner dolphins are true group-sex enthusiasts, engaging in orgies known as a "wuzzle." And some practice "beak-genital propulsion" or the insertion of the beak into the genital slit, pushing and penetrating as they swim together. Others engage in "genital buzzing," the use of vocalization, carried via sound waves in the water, to vibrate and stimulate the genitalia of their partners.

We transformed one particular sex act into the most show-stopping sculpture in the exhibition. It depicts Amazon river dolphins engaging in blowhole sex. Amazon river dolphins, called the boto, are typically eight feet long and weigh over 350 pounds. There's quite a bit of mythology surrounding these creatures, who are regarded by some as shape-shifters who can transform into humans and engage in intercourse with local women. This belief may originate from the human-like qualities of their genitalia and the pink tone of their skin. Although this legend remains a myth, we do know that botos participate in sexual relationships with another species of river dolphin known as the tucuxi.

While in captivity, two male Amazon river dolphins were documented engaging in blowhole penetrative intercourse. Though boto sexual encounters can last for hours, this particular act of penetration only lasted for one minute. Rune Olsen used this incredible interaction as the basis for his signature sculpture in the exhibition.

Same-sex relationships have long been documented in the Amazon river dolphin, as well as in over five hundred other animal species. Displays of affection, courtship, mounting, stimulation, pair bonding, and parenting behaviors between animals of the same sex have been documented in gray whales, giraffes, lions, fruit flies, koalas, African elephants, and the American bison, just to name a few.

At watering holes, male elephants may intertwine trunks, gently nudge each other, place their trunk tips together, or touch mouths in a "kiss." Males mount one another and participate in affectionate behaviors with visible erections. Captive female elephants have been observed masturbating one another using their trunks.

In the animal kingdom, homosexuality is not an anomaly and is not considered maladaptive. It's clear that animal homosexuality supports social bonding and the social infrastructure. And yet, until recently, homosexual behavior in animals was rarely documented. In some cases, this was due to scientific conservatism and concerns over reputation and funding. In others, the data may have been deemed insignificant. When recorded, these acts have been euphemistically referred to as "diddling," "necking," "cavorting," "rump-rubbing," and "penis fencing," terminology that fails to acknowledge the sexual nature of these interactions or their significance.

It's not that animals have suddenly decided to be "gay," it's that our perspectives, as well as our capacity to speak openly about sex, have changed with time. Biology may be rooted in the secular tradition of ancient Greek scholarship, but the field only became formalized as a science in the early 1800s—a time deeply ruled by Judeo-Christian doctrine in the Western world. Even Darwin's theory of evolution was not published for nearly twenty years due to an inhospitable social climate. And it's still not fully accepted to this day.

Many scientists have long documented same-sex relationships in animals, but this data was traditionally ignored, desexualized, or treated as anomaly—all difficult attitudes to justify when multiple pairs of male gray whales have been witnessed rubbing their eight-foot-long penises together. The sad truth is that *sex* is the one word that can even make scientists uncomfortable. The inclusion of those three little letters is a very quick way to get research grants and tenure applications denied.

Take the case of the homosexual necrophilic mallard. This astonishing event may never have entered the scientific record if Kees Moeliker, the curator of the Natural History Museum in Rotterdam, Holland, wasn't brave enough to publish his unusual observations in 2001. What could have been another day at the glass-faced Rotterdam Natural History Museum transformed when a male mallard (*Anas platyrhynchos*) crashed into the side of the museum, meeting his demise. Although mallards are known to have same-sex relationships, and in-flight rape is also common, Moeliker had no idea he would witness the first documented case of homosexual necrophilia as he left his office to collect the dead mallard.

Moeliker watched for an hour and fifteen minutes while a live male mallard mounted and copulated with the dead male, stopping only twice to dismount and rest. Necrophilia is perhaps not the most pleasant topic; still, consider the numerous coincidences that had to work together to bring this knowledge to us: A bird had to literally crash into a natural history museum and an expert on animals had to witness the incident *and* have the presence of mind to document it with photos. Then he spent six years mustering the courage to risk his entire career by publishing a scientific article on the observation.

Moeliker's observation did not go unrewarded. He gave a very popular TED Talk ("How a Dead Duck Changed My Life") that propelled him to nearly scientific rock star status. And in 2003, he won the Ig Nobel, an award based at Harvard University that honors science that "first makes you laugh, and then makes you think."

I hoped our exhibition would have the same effect on people.

→◆ ◆←

By the time *The Sex Lives of Animals* was set to open in July 2008, I had been researching for more than a year. The exhibition finally came together as a unique and coherent exploration of the illuminating truths about sex in the animal kingdom. But the process of building this one-of-a-kind exhibition had given me more than a unique education: its success validated all of my hopes for creating knowledge and opening minds. I realized that I had a job that made a difference in its own particular way. I was no longer intimidated by the ignorance of others, or upset by how their misconceptions might alter the way they treat me. I was proud to be the curator of the Museum of Sex, happy to answer the question, "What do you do?"

It seemed Jason felt the same way. Whereas my job used to feel like the dirty little secret in our relationship, he was now asking if he could get extra invites for his friends for the exhibition opening.

Before the party, we had a press preview, a two-hour window for the press to view the exhibition before it opened. It was like being at a cocktail party where everyone is trying to talk to the same three people: me, Joan Roughgarden, and Rune Olsen. I talked with every major news outlet in the city: *The New York Times,* Reuters, and the *New York Post.*

The *New York Post* ran a full-page photo of me, and for the first time, I was getting attention as an individual, not just as a spokesperson for the museum. (I began getting my share of letters from prison inmates asserting I was their soul mate. They loved animals as well, they said.) It was daunting, but kind of exciting. The next day, booking agents for the morning shows started calling. My first live, in-studio interview was *The Morning Show with Mike and Juliet* on Fox. I didn't have any formal media training. I didn't know exactly what I would be asked, but I felt confident enough in the material that I could handle whatever was thrown my way.

The first time Grandma saw me on TV, the topic was panda porn.

Yet despite all the press, the highlight for me was the opening-night party. The museum was packed with five hundred people and the guests were actually reading *all* of the exhibition text, not just the first few lines. This is the real measure of success for a curator, far more meaningful than any media.

Most gratifying of all was watching Jason share animal sex facts with a group in the corner, proudly announcing he was the curator's boyfriend, smiling cheekily at me as I walked past.

Maybe this is what emboldened me to do the one thing you are never supposed to do in a relationship: give an ultimatum.

fifteen

Beyoncé Said It Best

How much?" The man looked to see if he was being watched as he stopped me in the doorway of the museum.

I knew immediately that the "how much" referred to *me*—not to the museum exhibition. I'd dealt with this before, but mostly over the phone from callers who spoke to me as if they were on a sex chat line.

"This is a museum. For education," I said. "You can purchase a ticket in an hour when we open." I tried to sound authoritative and professional, though I sensed nothing would convince this guy that he wasn't standing outside a brothel.

"So how much?" he asked again, as if to challenge my coyness.

"An admission ticket is $17.50. As I said, this is a museum."

"Only $17.50!" he said, as if I was offering him the deal of a lifetime. But, almost as quickly, his delight transitioned to suspicion when he looked at the window display for *The Sex Lives of*

Animals. The glass was decorated in large font with factoids: frogs engage in group sex; manatees have been known to have sex in the 69 position; and, my personal favorite, female elephants can masturbate one another using their trunks.

"I'm not into the animals!" he told me.

I had to laugh. Did he really believe he was standing his ground against bestiality? Just as I was about to give him a more strongly worded explanation about the museum, one of my co-workers came up from the basement, and in her arms was our office cat, Tiger. The man completely freaked out. I guess the place no longer seemed so appealing.

→• •←

Although I understood that monogamy wasn't for everyone, I knew that was what I needed to keep participating in this relationship. But my job made me confront the very real possibility that this was an unrealistic goal.

I blamed the prairie vole.

The prairie vole has long been used as a model for human monogamy, a species, it was believed, that partnered for life. But that doesn't mean there isn't some sex on the side. Through DNA testing, scientists have discovered that the cute and cuddly prairie vole may have a different father than the expected pair-bond partner. Just like a paternity-test reveal on a television talk show, the father isn't always the person you are "monogamously" bound to. Mating for life apparently doesn't preclude getting pregnant by another partner.

And so an experiment was conducted. Three voles (a male and female pair bond and a "strange" female) were placed in a multicubicle domicile—think, laboratory version of a hamster hotel. Almost immediately the male scurried up to the unfamiliar female and tried to make a move, which was violently dismissed. Frightened and rejected, the male then hurried, with his tail literally and figuratively between his legs, over to his pair bond, or vole wife, snuggling into her. He may have remained technically faithful, but it wasn't for his lack of effort. We featured this video in the exhibition.

The more time I spent in the world of sex, the more I learned, and the more complicated the whole ball of romantic, interpersonal, social, biological, and historical dynamics became. I was fascinated by my work; nevertheless, all of this information muddled my thinking about personal relationships. But certain truths prevailed, and my major takeaway after all of these years working at the Museum of Sex was the undeniable power of our sexual desire.

Although sexuality, at its core, is filled with positivity and unlimited creativity, I have seen the many ways sexual desire comes into conflict with the social architecture of our society. I have seen too many people who, scared or embarrassed to share their kinks or desires with their partners, are driven to find satisfaction elsewhere. I have also seen the manifestation of the seven-year itch across the animal kingdom and the human sphere, sexual novelty winning out over monogamy. While the concept of the seven-year itch was immortalized in the 1955 film of the same name, in reality, some scientists have reported an even shorter *four*-year partnership cycle, dictated by the time it takes to birth a baby and care for it in the crucial first three years of life.

Neither theory left me optimistic about the odds of a lifelong romantic partnership.

The longer I worked at the museum, the more I wondered whether one person really could satisfy the desires of another. Although I wanted very much to have a traditional nuclear family, my job made me dubious. It's nerve-racking to doubt the one thing you've held as your ideal.

I had seen the little black books of too many escorts and dominatrices filled with endless names of married clients. I didn't want to be the wife who had no idea where her husband was, what he was doing, and whom he was doing it with. I'd been bombarded by research on porn addiction, sex addiction, and political scandals. It felt like every day I was coming across something at work that reminded me how the odds were stacked against those of us looking for monogamy. I mean, if those sweet little voles couldn't even be monogamous, did humans really have a better chance?

But I couldn't give up. I had to try. I wanted to try—with Jason.

At some point, in the midst of a crazy year, I had fallen in love.

Although the relationship had certainly flourished, it was still perplexing. It was like we were two different species thrown together, each trying to learn the language of the other. Often unsuccessfully. But I knew, in spite of all reason, that Jason was the person I wanted to spend the rest of my life with. He was my future. I knew what I wanted. A lifetime of chaos and upheaval had left me with an intense drive for "normalcy," and I couldn't settle for less.

Jason was already talking about bringing me back to Dublin for Christmas (without the suitcase full of sex toys this time), but I knew I couldn't do it without a commitment. Earlier that year Jason and I had had "the talk." We were exclusive, dating only each other, a relationship status that evolved only after many misunderstandings and arguments, often erupting around last call at the bar. But I wanted more and there was no point in spending the holidays with his family if Jason didn't see the same future I did. I had done this before with Nick and couldn't go through that pain again.

We were at a small tapas bar in Soho called Ñ, across the street from his apartment. We always ended our night there with one last drink. Just as Jason was paying the check, with my heart in my throat, I got up the nerve to say, "I love you. I want to have a family and I want to be with someone who wants all of that with me. So unless there is a ring on my finger, I won't be coming back to Dublin with you."

He seemed a little taken aback. But, as they say, there was no putting the genie back in the proverbial bottle. And so, for weeks, my uncomfortable declaration hung in the air between us. For some, my ultimatum might have seemed impulsive, but I was trying to learn from the past, and I was eager to protect my heart. I wanted Jason to be as certain about me as I was about him.

It was around this time that Beyoncé released "Single Ladies (Put a Ring on It)." A coincidence? A message from the universe? No matter what, I dutifully sang along.

—→◆ ◆←—

Despite the ultimatum, our relationship continued as normal. Jason and I were growing closer and discussing next steps, spurred on in part by Jason's decision to purchase an apartment, a big commitment for a foreigner. Although he said the three-bedroom apartment was an investment, I couldn't help but see it as a sign that he, too, was thinking about the future. And a family. But when we discussed a timetable for my moving in, I got little more than . . . "eventually."

In spite of his vagueness, we began the domestic activities of buying furniture and sheets. I had to explain to the bachelor why we needed to buy more than two bath towels.

Out on a voyage to a Brooklyn warehouse to choose furniture for Jason's new apartment, the one I hoped I would be living in sooner rather than later, we passed one of those quarter candy machines, the kind outside bodegas that sell gumballs and action figures. Jason put in a coin, and in return he got one of those turns-your-finger-green metal rings from a plastic capsule. Bending down on one knee in the middle of a street in Greenpoint, Brooklyn, he placed it on my hand.

Although not an official proposal, it was a gesture, one that I could tell meant *stick in this with me a little longer*. I was touched, but not placated. It was a step in the right direction, but as I looked down at the fluorescent purple stone on my hand, I knew it wasn't the real deal.

Burnt out from the adultness of furniture shopping, we moved on to Cafe Noir, a Sunday day drinking institution in New York with an eclectic mix of patrons—fashion girls, artists, corporate types—and bottomless pitchers of sangria. As one pitcher leads to two, it's the kind of place where you are certain to fall into conversation with strangers. As expected, the couple sitting next to us asked me the standard New York question, "So what do you do?"

Jason looked at me and smiled. "My lovely fiancée is the curator of the Museum of Sex."

sixteen

Romance with an Edge

When Jason asked me to accompany him on a work trip to L.A., two weeks after he had "proposed" outside of the bodega, I didn't really think much of it. He traveled a lot and I tried to go with him as often as possible. I didn't get suspicious when he insisted we visit one of his favorite places, Runyan Canyon, nor did I raise an eyebrow when he asked me if I would mind waiting in the car while he pulled over for a "quick errand" near the Beverly Center. But when we arrived in beautiful Runyan Canyon and he got down on one knee, I could barely process what was happening—and he could barely finish his sentence.

"I'm giving you this ring because it's titanium." With all of our ups and downs, for him, the symbolism of choosing a ring forged out of one of the strongest metals was deeply symbolic. "But we can go pick out a more traditional ring with a diamond together if that's what you want."

Already a hyperemotional person, I was powerless against the rush of emotion I had at the top of that canyon. On that beautiful rock, three time zones from New York, the museum, and all the other distractions in my life, I felt like I had finally come home. With Jason.

We still had to climb down from the canyon, but I don't remember a single step.

→◆ ◆←

Back in New York, the celebratory dinners and drinks continued. I was one of the first of my group of friends to get engaged, and as such, I found that my girlfriends were almost more excited than I was to get the wedding planning started (the wedding being an excuse for a great party and a chance to flirt with Jason's charming Irish friends).

Although my bridesmaids spanned a lifetime of friendships— from a childhood friend to a colleague from the museum—most were friends I had made during college. Leila, Cristina, and I, for example, formed an inseparable trio. I met Leila during my junior year (which was her senior year), and we liked to joke that we would likely have failed out of college had we met any sooner. After she graduated, Leila would drive the eight hours to Connecticut from her postcollege home in Montreal to pick up Cristina and me for a two-hour drive to NYC and a weekend of clubbing. Good times.

Cristina and I met earlier, during freshman orientation. We bonded over our bicultural backgrounds (Cristina's mother had met her father in Italy when she fled El Salvador during the civil war), which were in prominent, sometimes painful contrast to the New England prep school culture of Connecticut College. But it wasn't until we returned from studying abroad—me in Mexico and Hawaii, Cristina in Italy—that our friendship fully solidified. Reunited by the fate of a housing lottery, we ended up living next door to each other. For the next two years, we shared every meal, spent our evenings studying in tandem, and every day at five p.m. opened a bottle of cheap wine as we chatted, laughed, and cried about whatever was happening in our lives.

As close as any *hermanas,* Cristina and I planned to move in together after college, but her path took her to Berkeley to conduct research on immigration, which eventually led her to the Peace Corps and to Mali, where she had been stationed for the past two years. She was meant to be home shortly, but she had just extended her trip. With distance and time zones, we had only been able to exchange e-mails about the proposal and my request for her to be a bridesmaid. Just a day or two earlier I had gotten an excited voice-mail message from her: "Chica, I'm so, so happy for you! I can't wait for us to all be together celebrating. It's going to be the best homecoming ever." I remember the words, but more than anything what I remember—what I will always remember—was the pure love in her voice. She was so sincerely happy for me and so excited to share in that with me.

It would be just a short flight for her to get to Marrakesh.

After Cristina's voice mail came the call from my grandmother.

"You know, Sarah—sex is very important in a marriage."

I appreciated that she felt it her duty to break this news to me. Still, even with the explicit nature of my job, this phone call made me blush.

The pragmatic researcher in me wanted to approach this in a scientific way. In the ten months between engagement and marriage, I became the Grand Inquisitor of Sex. I wanted to work through a course of premarriage-sex communication, my own sex-heavy version of the Catholic Church's Pre-Cana. I didn't want to find out ten years into marriage that Jason was a closet furry or pony play enthusiast. We needed to get everything out on the table. Luckily, a close professional associate, Kimi Inch (also known as Mistress Nina Payne), offered the perfect opportunity with her Domi Dollz courses. In her quest to bring kink to the mainstream, Kimi and her dominatrix colleagues teach courses on everything from the basics of kink to the highest-level techniques and practices.

"Romance with an Edge" was a Valentine's Day special that was being held at the sex store Coco de Mer. The invitation described it as an "intimate salon that will inspire you and your partner to release all inhibitions and embrace that kinkier and playful side." I convinced Jason to come with me, even though he was particularly reluctant after seeing the invitation. He was not happy with the fine print, so to speak: "This is not a lecture, so don't expect to stay in your seat long! Sexy models to be used in demonstrations by instructor and attendants for a very intimate and interactive learning experience." I promised I wouldn't make him get on stage, though this wasn't really a promise I could keep. We would be at the mercy of Kimi.

Jason and I took the subway down to Elizabeth Street, where rows of fold-out chairs were set up in the back of the store.

"I'll be right back," I told Jason, leaving him to peruse the glass dildos that looked like something from a Murano shop in Venice. He was clearly uncomfortable, but I needed to find Kimi before things got started.

Kimi greeted me with a warm welcome.

"Can I ask you a favor?" I said. "I'm so happy I can be here to support you, but my fiancé . . . can you please not single us out or call us to the stage?"

She gave me a conspiratorial wink. Was that a yes? A no? I realized that deep down I was as nervous as Jason. Through my job I had been exposed to many starter sex courses, focusing on everything from blow jobs to burlesque techniques. But I was always there in a purely professional capacity. Here, with Jason, I felt the nervous butterflies most people feel when attending one of these events for the first time.

I was torn. On the one hand, I'd been reading for years about sex clubs and sex parties, eagerly devouring the exploits chronicled in *New York Magazine*'s sex diaries as well as the book it inspired, *The Sex Diaries Project*. I had also just finished reading *Live Nude Elf* by Reverend Jen, a performance artist known for wearing elf ears and not much else. The book detailed the author's adventures cleaning people's houses in the nude, signing up for slave training, and participating in orgies, and a memorable chapter outlined her journey learning how to "squirt." It was funny, smart, and outrageous—my new favorite sex book. I particularly related to Reverend Jen's discussion of how her job impacted her personal life. Not only was her book fair warning—sex with a sex writer means you never know when they might write about you—it was also a reminder that working in the sex field may not be conducive to fostering a traditional relationship. But unlike Reverend Jen, I had worked very hard over the years to build an ironclad wall between my personal and professional explorations.

So as I sat down for my indoctrination into Kimi's "Romance with an Edge," I reminded myself that this was an experience to have with Jason, not anthropological research for my next exhibit.

With a slave on hand for demonstrations, Kimi, Miss Mona

Rogers, and Miss Scandalicious proceeded with humor and intelligence, rather than intimidation. Instead of a sex show, we were treated to a fantastic introduction to the world of kink. After the demonstration on restraint and Japanese rope bondage, we were given silky black bondage rope to try on our partners. If you needed a few pointers, the latex-clad ladies would help you out. My favorite part of the class was the comprehensive kink worksheet, listing a multitude of kink fantasies, communities, and sex acts.

How did you feel about spanking?

Erotic tickling? Humiliation play?

Were any of these things something you wanted to do and try? Or were they something you just liked the idea of?

Jason was a good sport, but every so often he would shoot me a look that said, "How much longer?" Personally, I found every minute of the course valuable. I was convinced that when it came to sex, honesty and communication were key to making a monogamous relationship work. I am pretty certain monogamy is nearly impossible to maintain without an understanding of your partner's sexual thoughts. Obviously, one kink class isn't going to provide a road map to a lifetime of fidelity. My sex life with Jason would be an evolving conversation. But I knew one thing for sure: if you don't think you can get what you need at home, you are more likely to follow in the footsteps of the vole and find it elsewhere. So I wanted to know what my soon-to-be husband really wanted. And I also knew that marriage was a leap of faith, so I would need to put my work-induced skepticism on the shelf. I had to take a leap.

After the class, Jason and I ducked into a nearby bar for a much-needed cocktail. With drinks in hand, partly as a joke and partly because we were a little inspired, we filled out our kink worksheet. In the process, we learned far more about the others' tastes and inclinations than we had during any conversation over the years. It shouldn't have surprised me. Balanced communication, rather than shooting questions, always has better results, especially when it comes to sex. This is exactly why Kimi's classes are so valuable. And yet another reason why I love my job and all the provocative yet brilliant people it brings into my life.

→◆ ◆←

After years working at the museum, I still never knew who might reach out to me on any given day with an interesting discovery or new artifact; it's what continued to make my job so exciting. So the day I received an e-mail from a wonderful pop culture appraiser named Brian, I got that familiar hit of excitement.

He told me about the collection of Eva Norvind, a Russian princess turned actress turned famous New York dominatrix, who had recently passed away. Not only were they breaking up her dungeon, but rumors had surfaced that a notebook listing her powerful clients may lurk in its depths.

I knew nothing about this infamous, fascinating woman. And as Brian brought me into her world, I genuinely felt like I had missed out by not having met her.

Eva Norvind had been a gypsy of sorts. The daughter of a Russian prince and an artist mother, she moved to Mexico as a teenager and was nearly kicked out of the Catholic country for trying to promote birth control. A Playboy Bunny by the time she was eighteen, Eva eventually became a well-known actress and was considered the "Marilyn Monroe of Mexico." Eventually, she moved to New York and set up Taurel Associates as a safe space to act out erotic fantasies. Taurel was located in a towering office building in Midtown Manhattan, the kind of building filled with dentist offices and law firms. That behind one of those non-descript doors a place existed where you could be tied up, flogged, have your balls stretched, and be humiliated—whatever your fantasy dictated—only added to the intrigue.

After establishing Taurel Associates, Eva became both a film-maker and a student of forensic psychology. This new work even took her to the set of *The Thomas Crown Affair,* where she was hired as Rene Russo's consultant. The director wanted to make sure Rene had a believable, sexually assertive persona. Eva's eclectic, inspiring life came to an abrupt end at age sixty-two when she was caught in a heavy undercurrent at a beach in Huatulco, Mexico.

As the Taurel Associates dungeon was dismantled and the items gifted to some of Eva's closest friends and colleagues, I was able to select a few pieces to join the museum's permanent collection. Artifacts like Eva's give our patrons a peek inside a world they may never have known existed. They tell stories—of individuals, of time periods, and of changing beliefs.

I was touched when I was given one of Eva's whips. At first I refused, thinking a better tribute would be to pass on this important memento to someone who would use it, who would actually carry on Eva's sexually liberated legacy. But then I had a vision of myself, decades in the future, thinking back to my time at the Museum of Sex. I could hold this whip and remember the crazy adventures, the stories, and the incredible collectors who, like Eva, not only changed the way I viewed the world, but showed me the benefits of forging my own path, regardless of what anyone thought.

I accepted the whip with gratitude.

seventeen

Two Funerals and a Wedding

Jason and I knew we wanted a destination wedding. It was in our nature as a couple to travel and explore, to do the unexpected. The hard part was deciding where. After thinking about Spain and Italy, I suggested Morocco. My friend from college, Leila, was from Casablanca. I'd actually backpacked with her across the country—from the Sahara to the beaches of Agadir—for a few weeks during college. I had fallen in love with the country and its culture, in particular the magic that I felt existed in Marrakesh, the "Red City." With Jason's family and friends spread mostly across Dublin and London, Marrakesh would prove a short flight for many of the wedding guests. Nonetheless, it was a bold idea, and I was thrilled Jason was on board.

Our roles came naturally. I became the creative director, and Jason took on the part of project managing, navigating the mountain of logistics and negotiations. In this case the bride's family couldn't pay the tab for the fairy-tale wedding, and it was the groom who stepped in to execute my dream come true.

It was now a month after Jason proposed and we were already booking tickets for a February trip to Marrakesh, when we would visit venues, hoping to find a location for an intimate September wedding. I tended not to answer my personal phone at work, but when I saw it was Leila, I picked up. (Leila spoke French and Arabic, so she graciously offered to help research venues.) But when I answered the call, all I could hear were sobs.

I ducked out immediately, to the one little spot in the hallway where you could talk privately, away from the chaos.

"What's wrong, sweetie?"

"I got an e-mail about Cristina. She was working on a project in a nearby village. A water tower collapsed . . . Sarah—Cristina is dead."

The rest of the short conversation was a blur. My brain simply couldn't process the words. This just couldn't be real. Someone had to have made a mistake. Maybe she had just been hurt? Maybe it wasn't even her? I knew the floods of tears were about to come and I didn't want to be at work. I quickly told Lizzie what had happened and got myself out of the museum as fast as I could. Just out the door the tears came so heavy I couldn't see as I sprinted the four blocks to my apartment.

I still had her voice mail on my phone, excited about coming to the wedding. I listened to it over and over again.

→◆ ◆←

Two weeks later, I woke up from a vivid dream. My grandfather came to me, laughing and vibrant as always. We were standing underneath the Blue Whale at the American Museum of Natural History—the one he helped make so many years previously, the one he took me to visit often throughout my childhood, the one he said he made for me. He was saying good-bye, but he was so happy and clearly at peace.

I woke Jason. "I think my grandfather might have passed away," I said.

I turned on my phone and saw the ominous text from my mom. "Sarah, call me." She confirmed what I already somehow knew: Grandpa Marvin had passed during the night.

These two losses, back to back, felt almost like a cosmic rebuke for the happiness of my engagement. Just when I thought things were normal, when I could feel safe and secure, I was reminded how quickly they could change.

In the last few years before my grandfather's dementia had set in, he would often asked what I was working on. Wanting to spare him the details, I gave simple answers like "film" or "art"—or in one particular case, "burlesque." At this mention he perked up in a way I hadn't seen in years. He motioned me close with a sparkle in his blue eyes and sang in a near-whisper an old song about a burlesque theater and Queenie, the thrilling performer.

> *Take it off, take it off, cries a voice from the rear.*
> *Off, take it off, soon that's all you can hear . . .*

Turns out my grandfather was singing a song called "The Strip Polka," by Johnny Mercer, which came out in 1942. Grandpa Marvin would have only been fifteen years old at the time of this song's release, but even through the haze of old age and dementia, this memory had made him smile. In those last few years, his smiles meant everything to me.

→◆ ◆←

I recalled Grandpa Marvin's fondness for "The Strip Polka" sometime later, when I received a call about a woman named Mara Gaye.

Mara's daughter-in-law, Dorothy, was in the process of making estate planning arrangements for the terminally ill Mara when she discovered an extensive collection of costumes, documenting Mara's former life as a burlesque performer in the 1930s, the golden age of the profession.

Dorothy's initial call to the museum was exploratory: Were these items of value? Would the museum be interested in a donation? Sight unseen, I knew the answer was yes. Dorothy had described a collection that was as vast as it was diverse. Not only did it promise an intimate glimpse into one woman's life, it also offered a look into the incredible world of burlesque, a world that had seen a resurgence in popularity over the last few decades. Burlesque was more than just taking off clothing. It was an art: the art of the striptease.

The female burlesque performer has been entertaining, thrilling, and seducing for centuries. In the early 1800s, burlesque was a kind of comedic theater for working- and middle-class audiences that parodied the upper class in raucous British music halls, French concert saloons, and theaters across the United States. The dance techniques found in burlesque are derivative of other "scandalous" European dance traditions, such as ballet and cancan, each controversial in its time for giving audiences a peek at the undergarments respectable women kept hidden. By the turn of the nineteenth century, burlesque was not just a part of popular culture, it was an American institution.

From the 1860s onward, burlesque became increasingly more risqué. By the 1920s, burlesque performers were most well known for their "strip," teasing the audience as they worked down to little more than pasties and a G-string. One of the lesser-known pieces of the burlesque performer's costume is the merkin, a fancy name for a pubic wig. Merkins were first crafted by prostitutes in the 1400s to cover syphilis scars or shaved (usually to get rid of crabs) pubic hair. Burlesque performers used the merkin to fool men into thinking they were seeing more than they actually were. Nowadays, women can get a glorified merkin made of Swarovski crystals, otherwise known as the "vajazzle."

In the late nineteenth century, burlesque troupes started traveling around the United States, exposing small towns to the tease. Performers were allowed to display different amounts of skin based on local regulations. In some cities performers couldn't be seen actually removing clothing so they had to run off stage quickly, remove their bras or stockings, and run back on. Some states required pasties, while others did not. Some states required "granny panties" (a sign of moral decency), while others allowed women to slither down to nothing more than a jeweled G-string.

During the Great Depression, burlesque became an important and increasingly acceptable form of entertainment for middle- and lower-class patrons alike, providing a mental escape from tough times. However, as its popularity increased, its morality came under attack. New York banned burlesque in 1937, only increasing its fame in other cities throughout the United States. By World War II, the seductive, seminude female body was once again

deemed "respectable" as pinup photography and burlesque became expressions of patriotism, used to boost the morale of male
soldiers.

Mara Gaye enjoyed a long career as a professional showgirl,
dancer with the Radio City Rockettes, model, and burlesque
performer in the 1940s–60s. Mara performed at well-known
venues, like Minsky's, the Troc, the Hudson Theater, Empire Theater, Club Samoa, and the Clover Club during the last glory years
of the field. In the 1960s, Mara opened up an erotic mail-order
clothing line, Tana and Mara, with fellow dancer and fetish
model Tana Louise. Gaye posed in their lingerie, teaming up
with her photographer husband to capture her in various stages of
undress.

For over fifty years, Mara stockpiled every newspaper and
magazine spread where she was mentioned. She kept every sheet
of music she performed and a copy of every check she was paid
with. She kept all of her correspondence and her lipsticks, hair
combs, bottles of dye, costumes, undergarments, pasties, and
even the vanity from her dressing room. When Mara passed away,
we gave this impressive collection a safe home at the museum.
Each item was photographed, measured, and wrapped carefully
in archival materials, preserving it for the next generation. Mara's
hoarding worked to history's benefit. Through the objects she left
behind, we can re-create her story, and the broader story of burlesque in the mid-twentieth century.

American society changed drastically in the period after World
War II, along with available forms of entertainment. Many male
audience members wanted burlesque performers to become more
"hard-core," to keep up with the explicit sexuality found in print,
film, and popular fashion. Sexualized images of the female form

became increasingly voluptuous by the 1950s, popularized in a wide range of men's magazines like *Bare, The Male Point of View, Esquire,* and *Playboy.* As film and television gained new heights of popularity, burlesque was marginalized and made illicit, contributing to its decline. Changing ideas about sexuality and women's rights further pushed the boundaries of existing norms, and by the end of the 1960s, women were stripping off their bras with new intentions—those of liberation, rather than titillation. Second-wave feminism viewed burlesque and its descendants— go-go dancing, pole dancing, and lap dancing—as exploitative to women, thus dismissing it as an art form.

But in the 1990s the tradition experienced a revival, reinventing burlesque's golden age for modern audiences. Stripping how-to courses and neoburlesque troupes rapidly gained popularity with contemporary audiences through a nostalgic regard for the glamour and stylized femininity of the past. The Museum of Sex even added a burlesque class to its events schedule. Today, the Rockettes, Las Vegas showgirls, and modern "exotic dancers" draw on the techniques made popular by American burlesque at the turn of the twentieth century.

In 2011, I incorporated all of this into my exhibition *The Nudie Artist: Burlesque Revived,* featuring the photography of Leland Bobbé and the illustrations of Luma Rouge. The exhibit showcased the people who are making burlesque a robust contemporary performance scene today. Indeed, many of the performers featured in the exhibition have used their routines as a platform for feminist statements on the power of female sexuality. To them, it's about stripping on one's own terms. Even male performers have gotten in on the act with "boylesque," burlesque performed by men.

I was excited to finally feature Mara's collection, displayed in a beautifully lit glass case, alongside these contemporary portraits of the field, connecting a line between the past and the future of the art form. It felt good, and important, to honor Mara's life—and I knew how much it meant to her family. It was something I think Grandpa would have been proud of.

→◆ ◆←

Between losing Cristina and Grandpa, I had lost the desire to plan my wedding. Nor was my mind on work, as much as I tried to distract myself with it. Luckily for me, the museum was under construction—two new galleries and a brand-new Fifth Avenue entrance were planned—and that put any exhibitions on the back burner. Little by little, I tried to engage with the details of both work and wedding planning. I felt certain that Cristina and Grandpa would want me to be strong and move on, to celebrate the life Jason and I were making together.

It was time to get my wedding dress.

After years at the museum, I was very much aware of the role costumes play in our fantasies and ceremonies, and Mara's collection had certainly taught me the importance of picking the right outfit. Still, I wasn't really in the mind-set for the traditional wedding dress excursion, where I'd be popping champagne, surrounded by all the women in my life. Which is just as well, because, in the end, it was as if my dress found me.

One afternoon Jason and I were in Soho when a turn down Mercer Street led to a pop-up shop run by a fashion editor who was clearing out her closet. (It was early 2009 and the economic downturn had affected all sectors of society.) We wandered inside, and immediately I noticed a white silk dress from the 1930s.

It was sleek and simple, without any embellishment. The dress was perfect, as if made for me. No label or hint to its provenance, it was a mystery artifact from another time. Perfect for a curator. I'm normally a pretty superstitious person, but something about this dress felt like destiny. I certainly couldn't worry about the fact that the groom was seeing it before the wedding.

Nothing in my life was ever conventional. Why should wedding dress shopping be any different?

→♦ ♦←

We married twenty minutes outside of the city center of Marrakesh, in a place called the Palais Rhoul. Everything was coordinated with the help of a wedding planner on the ground. She was a *Vogue*-recommended, highly efficient woman who was clearly used to a very different sort of bride. "We can have you riding in on a camel," she suggested. An idea I was quick to pass on.

Jason and I chose to have a multifaith ceremony to represent the diversity of our identities. Father Simon, a Catholic priest from Ireland, officiated. (With an uncle who's a deacon and another who's a monk, Jason was well placed to enlist a family friend from the abbey.) Father Simon welcomed the incorporation of our cultures: an Irish loving cup, as well as the Jewish ketubah and breaking of the glass. I wore a mantilla in honor of my Mexican heritage, and Jason and I exchanged the traditional Mexican *arras,* or coins.

Without a father and without a grandfather, I made the decision to walk myself down that aisle. I knew my mother wanted to walk with me, but it felt important to give *myself* to Jason.

But when the moment arrived, I felt like my feminist gesture had been a big mistake. With a six foot four groom, I thought I could get away with the bright-blue six-inch heels I had chosen. Although I had practiced walking in them for weeks, I hadn't factored in the practical reality of the wedding venue. We were married outdoors, and my "aisle" was a lawn covered with Moroccan rugs. Very hippie-chic in vibe, it was completely impractical in heels. As each couple in the wedding party walked across the lawn, the rugs bunched over the thick grass. I was quickly dreading my walk to the alter. My musical cue began— "Somewhere Over the Rainbow" by Israel Kamakawiwo'ole— and as I looked up to see a hundred pairs of eyes on me, my shoes gave way. I wobbled for a moment. And just when I thought my crash was inevitable, I caught Jason's eye. I saw his smile and a look that in that moment made me feel like the most treasured woman in the world. By the grace of whatever god you believe in, I somehow managed to right myself.

The evening was more than I ever could have dreamed possible. A magical mixture of posh and bohemian, emotion and debauchery, it was a joyous celebration, with some guests staying up all night, drinking, dancing, and others skinny dipping in the hotel's pool around sunrise. I don't know if it was the romance in the air, the far-off destination, or the majority of the guests in their twenties and thirties, but love and lust became the theme of the night. There were more dalliances than there were single people. That only seemed a fitting end to the wedding of the curator of the Museum of Sex.

eighteen

Put It On, Before You Put It In

Soon after I returned from my honeymoon, I was invited to interview for Asylum AOL's show *Hot Girl, Cool Job.* It wasn't exactly *60 Minutes,* but I would be in good company. The show had recently featured a sword swallower, a sexy sommelier, and the former *Daily Show* correspondent, actress and model Olivia Munn. I knew it was a great way to gain attention for my work. The filming was similar to other on-camera pieces I had done, a typical walk-through of the museum and its exhibitions. I told them: "For me, it's really about creating exhibitions that are educational, that are fun and entertaining, and in the end, socially responsible. I am an incredibly pro-sex person. I want people to be having great sex, but I also want them to be having safer sex."

I went on to introduce the sculptures in *The Sex Lives of Animals* and to discuss the bonobos and the male Amazon river dolphins. After that it was on to the permanent collection, where I explained the infamous anti-onanism device and the crowd favorite, our RealDolls. I wanted to show the interactive quality of the installation, so I grabbed the penis on the male RealDoll. I always include this as part of my tour, to normalize the experience. If I, as curator, can't touch the doll penis without looking uncomfortable, what chance did our patrons have? Though no one had ever caught this on film. . . .

I felt good about the piece. The only thing that gave me pause was how excited the filmmakers seemed about the moment I grabbed the RealDoll's penis. I doubted Jason would find it quite so amusing, so I decided to warn him before the footage was posted online.

I brought it up casually over dinner, and my relaxed attitude must have worked because he didn't seem to think my news was a big deal. That's usually the type of thing Jason would find distasteful, and I should have known by his lack of commentary that he was distracted and hadn't fully registered what I was telling him.

When the video came out a few weeks later, I excitedly sent along the link. Proud of his new wife, Jason shared it with a few of his close office colleagues. All was going smoothly until the RealDoll scene. As my hand hovered over the silicone phallus and his colleagues gathered around the desk, he couldn't help but shout out, "Don't touch the cock!"

That's when my phone rang: "Did you really have to touch the cock?" my new husband asked. Not the best way to start out a conversation between partners. When I realized that Jason didn't love the idea of his wife touching a penis—not even a fake one—for the entertainment of millions of men (at least that was his perspective), I also realized that my marriage was going to have more of an adjustment curve than usual.

→◆ ◆←

It had been a big year, with great loss as well as great love. Eager to refocus at work, I was craving a project that was real and had substance. I wanted to curate something *meaningful,* and with that desire the seeds of the exhibition *Rubbers: The Life, History and Struggle of the Condom* were sown.

In approaching this exhibition, I looked at the objects and asked: What kind of larger story can we tell? At least from my perspective, that's the heart of any exhibition. I wanted to examine how and why people used condoms (as well as why not) and discovered that the answer was complex: sex education (disease and pregnancy prevention, of course), material innovation, and practical usage.

Repeated inquiries from journalists told me there was public interest in the topic, but how was I going to turn this one little object into the focus of a large-scale exhibition? And how was I going to convince Dan that it was worth the effort and the money it would take to make the exhibition?

Few people truly understand the enormous cost of an exhibition. Shipping a piece of art internationally can cost thousands of dollars. Some places have exorbitant lending fees. For every piece of art you want to show you have to construct a case or prepare a frame. The museum-quality materials for these alone can bankrupt an organization.

As a for-profit museum, the Museum of Sex needs to choose its exhibition topics carefully. Although we are happy to take curatorial risks (which we often do), and we pride ourselves on avoiding censoring ourselves in response to criticism, we also must aim to create exhibitions that have a large public draw. Our livelihood depends on it, as it does for the larger museums who receive millions of dollars in government funding and private sponsorship. Would *Rubbers* be enough? At first, Dan wasn't convinced, but with a small exhibition window coming up that needed to be filled, he somewhat begrudgingly took a chance on my vision. I would have five months (a blink of an eye in the museum world) to make it happen.

Sponsorship helps defray many of the exhibition costs at other museums, but over the years we had seen how difficult it was to get major companies to associate themselves with an institution that was so unapologetically about sex. Curators are not usually the ones who secure sponsorships—a different profession and skill set—but I knew that if I was going to make this exhibition all it could be, I was going to have to be a hustler. No one would believe in this exhibition with the same passion as I did. I would be its best advocate. As I learned on my first day at the museum, it's sink or swim. I knew that if I was going to dream, then I'd have to dream big. That meant Trojan, the biggest condom company in the United States.

After rounds and rounds of conversations, sales pitches and contracts, Trojan ended up being our golden ticket. I was a curator on a mission and I had just secured the biggest sponsorship the museum has ever received.

While it might seem an obvious fit—a condom company and a condom exhibition—what was truly important to them, and in the end what I believe was the deciding factor, was convincing them I would in fact do the highly nuanced topic justice. Something the company could be proud to be associated with. A week later the check arrived.

There had never been an exhibition this comprehensive about the history of the condom. In the end, I found a wonderful group of supporters, including MTV's Staying Alive Foundation, Gay Men's Health Crisis, and AIDS Service Center. I secured loans from institutions as diverse as the Dittrick Museum of Medical History to the American Folk Art Museum. The exhibition came together as a mixture of fine art, history, and science. We included an array of voices and perspectives.

Antique condom tins resembling small Altoid boxes were the first thing on display. These ornate and graphically dynamic objects were the go-to packaging for condoms in the early twentieth century. They're collectors' items now. Also on view in this section was a condom display case from a 1930s pharmacy, which had a "privacy door" to preserve the modesty of women and children who might be scandalized by even the sight of a condom. Times really were different.

Decades prior to this, condoms were a product of the underground, sold at brothels, picked up from a helpful barman, or, if you were bold, purchased from a mail-order company that advertised "male sheaths" or "French letters." These early condoms were typically made of animal intestines and fish bladders, the industry standard at the time. But it was risky business, as it was illegal to send condoms through the U.S. mail at the turn of the century—any family planning materials, in fact.

But our modesty had consequences. When American troops went off to World War I, they went without condoms. Wartime pamphlets warning people about the dangers of prostitution and "loose women" simply weren't effective enough, nor were the "pro-kits" the troops were provided instead. The content of these kits—gauze and soap—proved ineffective against chlamydia, syphilis, and gonorrhea. Every day nearly eighteen thousand soldiers were unable to report for duty because of sexually transmitted infections.

By World War II, condoms were seen as a critical military strategy, along with a new campaign: "Put it on, before you put it in."

Rubbers gave our patrons a sense of the condom's history as a tool of prevention and protection. And it also highlighted the multitude of art and advocacy that has been made since the devastating emergence of the HIV/AIDS pandemic. Posters from the Silence=Death campaign hung prominently. A pink triangle, a symbol used by gay activists in the 1970s (an adoption of the pink triangle used by Nazis to identify homosexuals in concentration camps), stood above the thought-provoking white text. This campaign, the creation of the organization ACT UP, declared that "silence about the oppression and annihilation of gay people, then and now, must be broken as a matter of our survival." According to ACT UP, it was a time when many actively protested "both taboos around safer sex and the unwillingness of some to resist societal injustice and governmental indifference."

Also on display was Japanese American print artist Masami Teraoka's 1980s and '90s AIDS series, which put condom use center stage. With great generosity, Teraoka made several of these large-scale works available for the exhibition. Nearby in the gallery, modern safe-sex public service announcements flicker as projections against the wall.

To ensure that visitors left knowing how to use a condom properly, we displayed a model of a penis, the kind educators use. It even "ejaculated," reminding people that properly removing a used condom is another important facet of safe sex.

I was so proud of everything in this exhibit, but if I had to pick a favorite piece from the exhibition it would have to be Adriana Bertini's couture condom cocktail dress, made from twelve hundred hand-dyed condoms and fashioned after the Valentino dresses of the 1960s. Adriana is one of the first artists I encountered at MoSex. As curator it fell on me to review all of the unsolicited submissions sent to the museum. Some are great. Some are dick pics. (Why do people think a naked snapshot instantly qualifies for display?) When I first started, I inherited boxes of similar submissions accrued during the museum's first two years. It was my task to write the many letters, politely telling people we weren't going to show their work. But in some rare cases, I'd come across something amazing. That was the case with Adriana. It had taken me almost eight years to find the right venue for her exquisite condom dresses, and I was thrilled when I finally got the chance in this exhibit.

Other interesting conceptual art pieces included the cruel condom—a condom crafted entirely out of chain mail and covered with spikes; trendy condoms from renowned designer Marc Jacobs; and *Condoments* by WEmake, functional salt and pepper shakers molded from condoms. And in a combination of beauty and levity, Randy Polumbo's glass condom sculptures, filled with LED light strips, literally lit up the room with whimsy.

Some pieces I found through chance, as was the case with the striking photography found within the pages of Leslie-Lohman Museum of Gay and Lesbian Art's quarterly magazine *The Archive*.

While flipping through it, one photo practically jumped off the page. It was of a man lying on his stomach with the conspicuous ring of a female condom coming out of his ass. I did a double take, not having known that some gay men use female condoms in anal sex. I included this in the exhibition with additional text from the photographer that describes the psychology behind the use of female condoms by homosexual men, which stems from a post-AIDS culture of fear. If I was learning something new, I knew it was something that needed to be included in the exhibition. It proved to be both a provocative and conversation-inspiring piece.

And even more provocative was a sculpture made entirely of used condoms set in resin. Artist Franko B created the sculpture by assembling gritty used condoms taken from the trash of the infamous Fist nightclub in London. Disgusting? Yes. Unforgettable? You bet.

When constructing the exhibition, I knew it would be important to ease patrons into the topic, which is why it was orchestrated to build from tame to shocking. Needless to say, neither the photo nor the used-condom piece was placed at the beginning.

Ultimately, the exhibition traced the evolution of the condom as an object of beauty, innovation, disease prevention, sexual liberation, and moral questioning—one little object with immense social value. Or at least a lot of loaded conversation.

I was thrilled when I found out the exhibition was going to be reviewed in *The New York Times* Sunday Art & Design section. I'd walked the reporter through the exhibition myself. He asked interesting questions, and I sensed he found the depth of the presentation dynamic. But this same reporter had a great poker face and had not been a fan of the *Kink* exhibition. I was nervous.

I woke up early that morning and went online to find the

review. The article was titled "Unrolled, Unbridled and Un-abashed." I held my breath until I came to the third paragraph. He called the exhibition "fascinating." I could breathe again. He wrote, "These commonplace objects—widely used and rarely spoken of, often seen but infrequently displayed—are icons of far more than the phallus." The article included a photograph of a 1930s condom dispenser we had on display. I felt vindicated. Not only did the exhibition mean a lot to the people who work in the field of sex education and sexual health, but museum critics were excited about it as well.

To celebrate the exhibit's success, a designer from *Playboy* offered to make copies of the condom dress for Jessica, the museum's publicist, and me to wear to the opening party. I figured it isn't every day a designer wants to make a dress specifically for you, particularly out of such an unusual material. I was excited about the idea, and told Jason as soon as I got home from work.

"So you are going to wear a dress made out of used condoms?" he said with undisguised irritation.

"Not *used* of course, just expired—condoms that can't be used anymore. Past their use-by date. Isn't that exciting?"

"Don't you think it's inappropriate for a married woman to wear a dress made out of used condoms?" he retorted, unable (and still unable to this day) to refer to them as "expired."

This dress would have been okay for single Sarah, but it was not okay for wife Sarah. I couldn't believe a condom dress had gotten Jason so upset, particularly after everything else he'd seen at my job. But maybe it was because of it, and he still wasn't thrilled I "touched the cock." Or perhaps coming from a Catholic country where condoms were illegal until 1978 (his parents had to travel to England to stock up) was what made a condom dress seem particularly transgressive.

Though I sometimes found these moments endearing, I didn't this time. My independence felt threatened. I knew compromise was important, but I didn't think it would manifest in this way. I never planned on being the kind of wife who needed to ask permission for anything. Certainly not the type of wife who could have her outfits vetoed.

I told Jason I would think about it, assuming with a little time he would relax. Could he really feel so strongly about something as minor as a dress? But as most arguments in marriages, it's not about the actual fight, it's about what it symbolizes.

I polled various people: Was wearing a condom dress something to be upset about? My respondents were split, and I was surprised when some of my more liberal friends said they too would have a problem with it, or at least they understood Jason's perspective. But more important, even if they couldn't, they reminded me, I needed be sensitive to our differing points of view. Wasn't this a part of what marriage was all about? Or any successful partnership for that matter?

In the end, I was saved from having to make a decision: as the date of the opening approached, the designer only had time to complete one of the dresses and I suggested Jessica be the one to wear it. Fate intervened. Of course it would have been fun, but was it worth hurting my husband who, in so many ways, had been patient with my profession, one that constantly pushed the limits of his comfort zone?

nineteen

Operation Baby Bump

Along with good reviews, the museum had attracted a celebrity following. One day, I got word that Jared Leto wanted to host a party at the museum. His band, Thirty Seconds to Mars, had recently had the video for its song "Hurricane" banned from MTV. Fetish imagery—nipple tassles, bondage hoods—will do that. So what better place to show the video and celebrate its censorship than the Museum of Sex?

Jared came to check out the space for himself.

Not only was I giving a sexually explicit tour to a celebrity (always a little unsettling), but I happened to be giving that very tour to the object of my eleven-year-old Jordan Catalano fantasies. While Leto has gone on to become an Academy Award–winning actor, for me he will always be Claire Danes's love obsession in the '90s television show *My So-Called Life*. I tried to remind myself that I was no longer that girl, but a grown married woman—and a professional one at that. I could do this.

Jared arrived wearing a poncho and a very California vibe—half-distracted, half-daydreaming. The tour was brief. We didn't talk much beyond my bringing to his attention various types of porn, sexual apparatuses, and the vintage vibrators on display. He nodded his head a few times. Was I boring him or was I just paranoid? Still, he must have been impressed enough because he ended up hosting the party at the museum.

And yet, while the Jared Leto tour was memorable, it was not the top of my celebrity encounters list. That spot belongs to musician Tommy Lee. Lee had his own place in the pantheon of sexual history thanks to his infamous sex tape with Pamela Anderson.

When Tommy stopped by the museum, his film crew was in tow. He was working on the Methods of Mayhem album *A Public Disservice Announcement.* He, too, thought a visit to the Museum of Sex would be a perfect publicity tie-in for his album. I was dubious at first, but he turned out to be the loveliest guy.

I met him while he browsed the gift shop. (He seemed particularly excited by the *Cunt Coloring Book,* which is pretty much exactly what it sounds like.) I suggested we go upstairs to the first gallery, our *Spotlight on the Permanent Collection.* Like a sampler box of chocolates, the spotlight gallery would expose him to an eclectic assortment of artifacts: RealDolls, bondage equipment, and a Fuck Bike.

We began at the Fuck Bike #001.

"I have one of these," he said. For all I knew this wasn't a joke.

Turning eagerly to see the next artifact, Tommy reached out to touch the St. Andrew's Cross, the large X-shaped bondage structure, formerly installed in Domina M.'s dungeon. Half of New York had been bound to this cross at one time, and here was Tommy Lee, posing with it.

But then an inflation video caught his eye. Seeing his confusion I explained. "This guy is having saline injected into his scrotum."

"Saline?" he said. I got the feeling that the guy who has seen and done it all (and much of it on film) was learning something new. Grad school had not prepared me for this kind of exchange. I could feel myself blushing.

"You need to really know what you're doing with medical play," I told him.

"So this is . . . temporary?"

"Yes. It will all be reabsorbed into the body."

"Whoa," he said. "Boy—you learn something new every day!"

We moved on to *Action: Sex and the Moving Image* and some of the vintage porn clips.

"As soon as people had a camera, they were taking naked pictures," I told him. "This first one is from 1915."

"1915? Was this like a full-on porno, or just light porn?" he asked.

"No—it's full-on. It's as hard-core as anything they're doing today. Anything you can imagine, they were doing."

"Whoa. 1915. That's a long time. That's a lot of horniness."

There was just one problem. I realized as we moved toward the room with *Sex and the Moving Image* that one wall had a giant projection of Tommy getting a blow job from Pamela Anderson, a clip from their infamous sex tape. I didn't think he'd be upset, but I didn't particularly want to stand there and watch it with him. I was open-minded, but that was definitely pushing the limits of my comfort zone! I hustled him through, praying he wouldn't notice. Miraculously, he didn't.

And then it was on to *The Sex Lives of Animals*. We stopped in front of the statue of two female bonobos locked in passion.

"This is called the g-g rubbing: genito-to-genito rubbing."

"That's two females?"

"Yes. This is a common sexual act for females. Their clitorises are about two and a half inches long, so they can actually penetrate one another."

We looked at photos of a snake.

"They have two penises," I said. Technically, these are called hemipenes.

"Party," said Tommy.

In the next room, the condom exhibition, Tommy stopped in front of a public service announcement, a photo of a beautiful blonde wearing only black panties and stilettos. She was on her knees giving a guy a blow job. But instead of putting a penis in her mouth, she had her lips around a gun that jutted out from where the guy's penis should be.

"Oh, what a great shot! That's cool."

Afterward, he tweeted, "What a spot!! when in NYC ya'll must visit!! thanks guys . . . even I learned a few thangs!"

If I could educate a rock star with a famous sex tape, I really must be doing something right.

→• •←

The museum was coming up on its first decade and was experiencing tremendous growth. With two new galleries to fill, the upcoming year would prove to be complete and utter madness. Already in the works were three large-scale exhibitions: *Comics Stripped, Nudie Artist: Burlesque Revived,* and *Obscene Diary: The Secret Archive of Samuel Steward—Professor, Tattoo Artist and Pornographer.* This would be no small feat, and more than three times the workload of the average curator in the same time frame. And

I didn't just have work on my mind: Jason and I wanted to start a family.

After years of devoting my time to the study of recreational sex, my focus turned to that other kind of sex: procreational. Operation Baby Bump was officially under way, and it was the first time I really needed my professional knowledge to inform my personal life.

I began my road to pregnancy a year after Jason and I were married, making the deliberate decision to stop using birth control pills. Some of us spend so much of our young adult years using contraception that we think if someone breathes on you the wrong way, poof, you get pregnant. Although true for some, for me at least, that wasn't the case.

Sex is my area of expertise, and, at twenty-eight, I had youth on my side; nevertheless, I spent months trying to conceive with no results. It wasn't just frustrating, it felt like a reproach of my femininity, and a burden on my marriage. I replayed the technical facts in my mind, as if an intellectual approach could help. I knew that some scientists believe the female orgasm to be an evolutionary adaptation to aid in conception, and that the contractions experienced during orgasm can actually "upsuck" (scientific term) the semen to the ever-eager egg. I knew about semen production cycles: best not to have sex every day, which just diminishes the stash of strong swimmers. And I knew about fertility-centric acupuncturists, menstrual cycles, and even the oh-so-glamorous world of cervical mucus. Yet none of this knowledge made me conceive any faster.

During this whole frustrating process, it struck me that so many women know so little about their bodies—and not just from a sexual perspective. How many women know how the ovulation cycle really works, or how to read various other signals that our bodies give us? I had been on birth control for a decade, and now the delay in conception made me realize we don't really know how manipulating our hormones affects us in the short term and long term. It took me eight months to have a normal period.

With as much as I'd learned about human sexuality, trying to conceive posed a whole new set of questions. In many cultures, women pass this information down from generation to generation. But typically, this is not a conversation that most women growing up in the United States today would have with their mothers. Generations ago, women were surrounded by others in the community when they gave birth. Today, some women hire doulas—professionals who provide encouragement and comfort, someone to rub your back and supply words of support—a role that used to be filled naturally from within the community. Most of us don't operate in that kind of system anymore.

The year mark of "trying" quickly approached. At this point doctors were willing to intervene and give nature a little nudge, but Jason and I decided to try for one more month without intervention. In the meantime, I also needed to stay focused on work.

→◆ ◆←

Although previous exhibitions had touched upon the subject of erotic illustration, it was becoming clear that cartoons, comics, and animation had become important enough to merit an entire exhibition. Not only did Marge Simpson appear on the 2009 cover of *Playboy,* but in 2010 Vivid Entertainment created VividXXXSuperheros, an imprint that produced porn parodies of popular comic characters such as Batman, Superman, Spider-Man, Ironman, and the Incredible Hulk. They even launched their own Vivid hero, Spread Eagle, in 2011. I was overwhelmed by the abundance of material.

For this project, which would come to be called *Comics Stripped,* I teamed up with comic historian Craig Yoe. Yoe had been recruited by Jim Henson as creative director and later VP/ general manager of *The Muppets,* and he was responsible for the development of classic toys like Cabbage Patch Kids and My Little Pony. He's also a cofounder of YOE! Studio with Clizia Gussoni. Craig knows his comic history. He became an incredible tutor, filling in the gaps left by my minimal comic education.

My "training" would begin at Comic-Con, the largest convention dedicated to comics, graphic novels, anime, manga, video games, toys, and animated film. Manhattan's Javits Center was packed for the event; the air buzzed with excitement as massive lines formed at each booth. I can't tell you how refreshing it was to see artists getting the attention typically reserved for rock stars and movie stars.

Yet, while I was prepared for the elaborate costuming, diversity of subcultures, and sexually charged environment, I wasn't prepared for what I experienced. Comic-Con draws many devoted female fans (and the number grows each year); still, women at this convention were dramatically outnumbered by the thousands of men. The attention was overwhelming.

But it was an awesome event and I was able to conduct a little participant observation—the field approach of anthropology— which led to tips on some Web sites that might help my education. I was shocked to discover how many cartoon porn sites showcase beloved characters in unbelievably compromising positions. I doubt I will ever be able to shake the image of my favorite childhood mermaid, Ariel, performing oral sex. But "dirty" drawings did not begin with the Internet; erotic illustrations can be traced back centuries.

Although we could have begun with cave paintings, our inquiry would start with the Great Depression, when comics were viewed as a harmless distraction from the everyday grind. Due to economic pressures, many mainstream comic artists moonlighted their talents for the production of erotic content. Small comic booklets known as Tijuana bibles or eight-pagers parodied characters like Blondie, Dick Tracy, Olive Oyl, and Wimpy, as well as Disney icons Donald Duck and Snow White and the Seven Dwarves, by placing them in erotic scenarios.

Although Wesley Morse is best known as the creator of the *Bazooka Joe and His Gang* comic that adorned Topps bubble gum, he was also one of the most well-known cartoonists of the Tijuana bible genre. And the crossover between the erotic and the mainstream did not end there. During the Depression, Joe Shuster of Superman fame crafted risqué artwork that featured busty women, fetishes, bondage, homosexuality, and other explicit encounters. One of his erotic series, *Nights of Horror,* depicts Superman and Lois Lane lookalikes in BDSM scenarios. By the early 1950s, erotic comics were a popular feature in men's magazines. Hugh Hefner, who once dreamed of becoming a comic artist, showed his reverence for the genre by including bawdy cartoons in *Playboy*. But with the advent of McCarthyism, the 1950s saw renewed censorship and nothing was safe—not even comics.

The Comics Code Authority was created to regulate the content of the field and determine what was and wasn't acceptable for publication. It led to a long-lasting form of censorship, similar to the Hays Code, which regulated motion pictures. The code dictated what could be sold at newsstands and comic shops for decades. Thus, the erotic was pushed to the underground, and erotic comic artists lived in fear of arrest.

Although publications like *Playboy* were able to push boundaries and include erotic comic series, such as *Little Annie Fanny* and Jack Cole and Eldon Dedini's watercolor depictions of horny satyrs chasing voluptuous nymphs, comics of this tone were hard to find elsewhere until the 1970s. Today, original panels of *Playboy*'s erotic comics are highly collectable art pieces and a lucrative investment. Some have sold at auction for thousands of dollars. Craig and I were thrilled when Playboy Enterprises agreed to loan us a wealth of original panels from their permanent collection for the *Comics Stripped* exhibition.

Playboy, and similar publications, remained a unique resource for erotic comics until the birth of the comix movement, a name synthesized from the fusion of "comics" and "sex," in the 1970s. Eager to circumvent the limitations of the Comics Code, the comix movement actively sought out alternative channels of distribution. Turning to underground vice culture, explicit comics found an outlet next to drug paraphernalia, mostly marijuana, at "head shops." Sexually explicit comics melded with the liberated ethos of such spots in the '60s and '70s.

Artist Robert Dennis Crumb, best known by the moniker R. Crumb, was one of the originators of the comix movement, with work that featured dominant women of "Amazonian" proportions. He's considered one of the greatest cartoonists of all time, and his participation in the comix movement served as inspiration for many other talented artists to join the fray. Another artist who pushed boundaries was *MAD Magazine* cartoonist Wally Wood; in 1967 Wood created the "Disneyland Memorial Orgy," published in *The Realist*. This detachable centerfold poster featured a mélange of Disney sexuality. Some highlights of the infamous work include a scene of the Seven Dwarves pulling off Snow White's clothing, eager to engage in aggressive group sex; a boldly curious Donald Duck pulling up the skirt of Daisy Duck from behind; a sex worker Minnie Mouse being penetrated by Goofy; and a stripping Tinkerbell. Pinocchio observes all this with a highly erect nose, alongside a drooling Captain Hook, Peter Pan, and Jiminy Cricket.

Yet the power of the comix movement wasn't just in parodying and representing graphic concepts. It was also about embracing all forms of sexuality. Homosexuality was well represented within the comix movement thanks to artist Touko Laaksonen, better known as Tom of Finland; Laaksonen is creator of some of the most iconic images of sexy, leather-clad motorcycle men. But same-sex relationships did not reach the comic mainstream until the 1990s when the presence of LGBT comic characters became an acceptable part of the illustrated tapestry. Another milestone was reached in September 2010 with the premiere of Kevin Keller in "Veronica #202," the first openly gay character in the Archie comics, one of America's longest running comic series.

The world over, erotic illustrations and images are meant to be a turn-on.

Previously, in our exhibition *Peeping, Probing and Porn: Four Centuries of Graphic Sex in Japan,* the museum had explored Japan's genre of erotic illustrations known as *shunga*. These hand-printed wood-block images were once sold in the *yoshiwara,* or pleasure district. *Shunga,* as well as its contemporary comic descendants manga (typically printed books) and anime (hand-drawn or computer-animated images), are often described as *hentai* if sexual in nature. Manga, which does not always focus on sex, is consumed all over the world, making it a unbelievably lucrative form of illustration. A global turn-on for certain (based on world popularity and sales), *hentai* caters to a wide range of erotic fantasies.

As Tom of Finland famously said, "If I don't have an erection when I'm doing a drawing, I know it's no good." This phrase has become a useful metric for generations of erotic artists whose fantasies are found splayed across the printed page for their reader's enjoyment.

As with my research for so many projects, I turned to collectors to help me round out this exhibition. And this time, I was met with one of my biggest challenges.

I've dealt with some protective collectors in my time, but J. B. Rund was the toughest of them all. Rund had a huge collection of John Willie fetish illustrations. Willie was publisher of the cult magazine *Bizarre,* one of the first to cater to the American fetish community. He created a series of bondage comic strips, the best known of which was *Sweet Gwendoline.*

Rund has referred to Willie as the Rembrandt of Pulp, as he was the first fetish artist to illustrate from models or his own photographs. According to a *Salon* profile, Rund spent years trying to get his work published. He eventually decided to do it himself and founded Belier Press in the mid-1970s. *The Adventures of Sweet Gwendoline* sold twenty-six thousand copies. Belier Press later published the first books about 1950s pinup queen Bettie Page, as well as underground cartoonists such as R. Crumb and Art Spiegelman, creator of the Maus series. It would be a coup for me to get something from his collection into the exhibit.

I met Rund at his apartment, a few blocks from the museum.

Although many of the collectors I worked with were initially suspicious of the museum's intentions, J. B. Rund was by far the most cautious. He was extremely protective of his possessions, his attachment both personal and professional. His interest in bondage, a fetish that emerged when he was twelve and playing a game of cowboys and Indians, was no secret. According to one book on Bettie Page, tying up the neighborhood kids caused a new sort of arousal. During his adolescence in the late '50s, he saved money to buy Bettie Page bondage photographs, which he kept safely hidden under his bed.

Belier Press was successful, but Rund was constantly battling against infringement and piracy of his copyrights. This legacy made it tough to gain his trust. It took several visits to convince him to exhibit a few iconic images of *Sweet Gwendoline*—drawings of bound women in six-inch heels—though he still kept us waiting until the very last minute to give the final go ahead. It was stressful.

Our *Comics Stripped* exhibition featured more than 150 artifacts telling the sexual history of the comic art form, one deeply valued by various kink communities. The medium has the power to make fantasies a reality. While porn provides the ultimate fantasy to millions of people, at the end of the day, videos and photographs are limited to the real-life constraints of human bodies. Some fantasies can only be brought to life with the help of a sympathetic illustrator or cartoonist.

Some people just need their comics stripped.

→◆ ◆←

When I wasn't sitting with comic book collectors (many of whom were very excited a young woman was displaying so much interest in their treasures), I was taking my temperature and peeing on ovulation sticks, my new morning routine. I recorded all data in my handy "get pregnant" app. In February 2011, a month after *Comics Stripped* opened to the public, I went off to L.A. for a girls' weekend. My ovulation window that month had just closed. I wasn't feeling myself—I was unbelievably thirsty and tired, not to mention tired of having to pee all the time—but it didn't occur to me I was pregnant. Though we had been trying, I didn't think it was possible to have the symptoms of pregnancy this fast. Instead, I convinced myself I was developing diabetes. All those terrible sour candies I eat like an elementary school kid were finally catching up with me.

When I landed back in New York on Valentine's Day, I decided to take a routine pregnancy test.

After all those months of waiting and frustration, after failing to see those coveted double lines, all of a sudden there they were! I was pregnant. And despite all of my efforts—or maybe because of them—I couldn't have been more surprised.

Jason had already left for work. I wanted to tell him in person, but I didn't know what I'd say. Pondering this, I went about my errands for the day, which included picking up dog food at the pet store. (Our Shiba Inu, She-ra, joined our family that year, a proxy for the pregnancy that hadn't taken hold.) There, I saw tree frogs for sale. And I knew how I'd deliver my incredible news.

A month or two earlier, consumed with the thought of having a child, I'd had a dream in which I was trying to catch a group of little frogs. I told Jason about my weird frog dream, and that it would be considered a pregnancy omen in many parts of the world. We were so eager for encouragement that we took it as a good sign.

Standing at the pet store that afternoon, my dream came back to me. So I bought a little terrarium and four frogs—one for me, one for Jason, one for our dog . . . and one for the baby. It's not that I needed an exhibit to deliver the news of our much wanted pregnancy, but why not take advantage of serendipity?

That night, when we were getting ready to go out for dinner, he told me that while I had been in L.A. he had been working on a project for me. "I know you don't think of me as a creative person, but I made you a painting," he said with such pride and excitement. It was a giant oil painting with bold red strokes across a canvas, and in the upper-left-hand corner was a small green frog. "I thought maybe this would bring us good luck," he said. I was floored. "Wait here," I told him and rushed to get the terrarium. He laughed, and we kissed and I had tears in my eyes. Jason thought I was emotional because we had been so like-minded. And then I told him, "I have some news. We're having a baby." It was intense and beautiful, another of those moments in life that made me think about fate. You meet a random guy in a bar, and the next thing you know you're dreaming about frogs and having a baby. My life continued to feel like a journey of adventure and the unexpected.

twenty

The Power of the Yoni

I was amazed by how societal boundaries fell to the wayside during my pregnancy. Maybe it was the anthropologist in me, but I was fascinated by the way people would just come out and ask pointed questions about the time, location, and position of conception. Some would even remind me to do my Kegels to ensure a "toned" vagina postdelivery. And of course, all my kink research made me acutely aware of pregnancy fetishists. My ever-growing breasts and belly were attracting more attention than I was comfortable with.

I thought a lot about my old friends Masters and Johnson. Before their research, having sex during pregnancy was thought to be unhealthy. Today it is not uncommon for couples to lead healthy, even voracious sexual lives right up until D-day. Some doctors, such as mine, even recommend having sex in the latest stages of pregnancy. The prostaglandins present in semen can help soften the cervix, inducing labor. Similarly, orgasm causes a release of oxytocin, the same hormone that causes contractions. Many baby preparation books now include sections dedicated to sex during pregnancy.

While some women lose their sexual desire, just as many will experience libido overdrive. Sometimes this is due to increased blood flow to the genital region resulting in increased sensitivity, or surges in hormones. And as the old wives' tale goes, a pregnant mother eager for sex is supposedly carrying a son. As the body grows, however, some serious geometry, flexibility, and humor must be utilized to do the deed. I can say that it was, by far, the least acrobatic time of my life.

For me, talking about other people's bodies and sex lives was second nature, but I wasn't used to talking about my own so freely. Although I threw out the words *vagina* and *vulva* on an almost hourly basis, it made me uncomfortable to use them about my own body.

The vagina, the vulva—or yoni; yonic can be used as the female counterpart of phallic—is confusing for many, even for a curator of sex. Artist Jamie McCartney's *Great Wall of Vagina*, composed of plaster casts from more than four hundred women, provides a visual representation for just how diverse the yoni can be. Then, of course, there are designer vaginas, merkins, and artificial hymens—used in various parts of the world to fake virginity. It's dizzying terrain.

The vagina artifact that shocked me the most in my years of research was an inflated rubber tube, known as a pessary ring, used to hold a vagina in. That's right: *hold a vagina in*. In extreme cases, when the pelvic muscles that surround the vagina are damaged and weakened, the muscle tissue can collapse, causing an elephant-trunk-like appendage to distend between a woman's legs. This is called a prolapsed vagina. It was once more preva-lent when maternal health wasn't well developed and women had many more babies. It's less frequent now, but the condition still exists. Thankfully modern medicine has developed other tech-niques to mend the yoni, though, in rare cases, the vagina ring is still used. For the past ten years, I've been fascinated and dis-turbed by this particular bit of anatomical information. I never get tired of sharing this shocking information with my friends—though none of them seemed particularly pleased to find out their vaginas could fall out.

I watched excitedly as my belly grew over the next forty weeks. As the first of my friends to get pregnant, my yoni was on a dif-ferent journey from all of the women in my life. I was the guinea pig, expected to return with information from the trenches, pack-aged for consumption like all the other sex facts I had acquired over the years.

→• •←

On my way to the labor and delivery room, I demanded that my husband keep his eyes in the "northern hemisphere" at all times (I'd heard the statistics about labor-induced bowel movements). Of course, my modesty soon disappeared in a cloud of pain and adrenaline. I was in the throes of an unmedicated labor and couldn't have cared less who was looking at my vagina. Jason stayed with me through every push and contraction. He was very kind and supportive, but he didn't listen to my dictate that he stay in the northern hemisphere. I'm betting he wished he did, though, when our son, Kai, emerged hand first, like Superman. I'll never forget the look on Jason's face.

As a new mother, every day brought discovery and wonder as

I embraced my new self, new status, and new body, every shred of modesty evaporated. Though I have always been comfortable in my skin, I wasn't the type to spend much time publicly naked, save going topless on a European beach. Yet the day after my son was born I was sitting in a breast-feeding class, bare breasted, with a group of ten women I had never met before. It took me a while to negotiate how to breast-feed in front of the people in my life. A hungry baby waits for no one, and so my husband's friends, and even my father-in-law, eventually saw my breasts.

I knew, from a sociological standpoint, that having a community was important during this wonderful but challenging time. So I decided to join a new mothers' group, where I found myself, once again, topless, talking about vaginas. Suddenly, it was perfectly normal to ask someone you barely knew: Did you tear? Did you have an episiotomy? How's your vagina rehab going? (For some women, the vagina needs to be reacclimated following childbirth with a course of vagina physical therapy and dilators.) What's your postpartum sex life like? You mean you, too, accidentally squirted breast milk on your husband's face during sex?

I was a little worried about what the new women in my life would think about my profession. Could the conversation accommodate both teething rings and cock rings? I needn't have been concerned. In fact, my MoSex experience quickly proved useful.

Kelley, who would become one of my closest mama friends, shared with the group her recent unusual encounter. After giving birth to a premature baby, one who was only able to consume a small amount of her ample breast milk, her fridge had quickly become overrun. Full of more than a thousand ounces of milk (the equivalent of 62.5 pounds; if gold, it would be worth approximately $1.2 million), she decided she would try and donate her "liquid gold," as breast milk is often referred to, to a family in need. It's a valuable commodity for adoptive parents and those having difficulties producing their own milk. She placed an ad within our mother board, but she also placed one on Craigslist, stating:

> I am a breastfeeding mother of an infant son with a large surplus of milk, mostly frozen. I am running out of storage room and would love to share with a family in need of milk. I am a healthy, non-smoking, non-drug-using mother who is pumping exclusively for my premature son. I don't have time to go through appropriate donation channels while my son is in the NICU but would hate to see it go to waste. Please contact me if interested.

It wasn't long before she got a response.

> Hi. Would you consider a wet nursing relationship with a very well educated groomed cultured male? I seek the emotional and psychological satisfaction . . . nothing more. Making a very respectful and considerate offer. Will be generous as well.

Now this was something in my wheelhouse. After a lively conversation, one of my new mama friends left with a copy of *Deviant Desires* tucked into the bottom of her stroller.

My fears of being considered a social pariah proved unfounded. It was sex, after all, that had led us each down the path to motherhood.

twenty-one

Mama Works in Sex

Like many women in the United States, I returned to work three months after my child was born. I'd haul my giant breast pump to work and, every few hours, sit in a cold closet turned pumping room, trying to keep up my supply. It was less than ideal, but I was lucky because the museum allowed me to find my own work-life balance—three days at Mo-Sex, two days home with my son. It was quite the juxtaposition. And I still needed to come up with exhibitions. Luckily for me, I had come across a great idea while resting prior to the birth of my son when, there on the nightstand, right next to *What to Expect When You're Expecting,* I came across a copy of *A Billion Wicked Thoughts: What the Internet Tells Us About Sexual Relationships.* (What can I say? I often took my work home with me.)

The authors of *A Billion Wicked Thoughts,* Ogi Ogas and Sai Gaddam, are neuroscientists who have studied over a billion online search queries, with some very interesting results. Basically, the authors' research determined that although pornography may be more accessible than at any other point in history, and although every possible niche has some kind of online representation, 80 percent of people look for online pornography in only twenty different categories. In short, most people's sexual fantasies are more similar than not.

Completely fascinated by the findings of this book, I pitched the idea of turning it into an exhibition that would open just one month after I returned back to work. *A Billion Wicked Thoughts* would become the *Universe of Desire: Why We Like What We Like.*

Type. Swipe. Search. Upload. Download. Post. Stream. These are the new verbs of desire. Our most intimate thoughts, fantasies, and urges are now transmitted via electronic devices to rapt audiences all over the world. These transmissions— from sexts to webcam masturbation feeds—are anonymous yet personal, individual yet collective, everywhere and nowhere, and they are contributing to the largest sexual record to date. In short, desire has gone viral. But what does this mean? And what does it reveal about us? This exhibition explores these very questions through a lens of digital experience by examining what we are searching for, how we do it and what we leave behind on these electronic devices. In piecing this together, we begin to expose staggering truths about who we are and how we interact in this ever-changing world of modern sexuality.

A Billion Wicked Thoughts unveiled the top ten online erotic search categories: youth (not pedophilia, think more "barely legal"), gay, MILFs (a term that took on a whole new meaning for me), breasts, cheating wives, vaginas, penises, amateurs, mature, and animation. Rounding out the top twenty were domination/ submission, incest, lesbian, black, bestiality, fat, transsexuals, anal sex, and grannies, in descending popularity.

It turns out that porn searches follow a predictable pattern in the way they showcase the various kinks and sexual preferences that pervade our culture: celebrities (#23), Asian (#29), water sports (#35), babysitter (#75), face sitting (#83), and gagging (#100). Some online searchers look for *squick,* or sexual content that is shocking rather than directly titillating. These images evoke a visceral response rather than immediate sexual arousal. But for some, this feeling is one and the same.

Although sexuality can be quite complex, for the most part, people search for pornography that centers on age and eroticized body parts. Many academics chalk this up to how our brains work: we tend to appraise someone's attractiveness based on the aesthetics of the face, the chest region, the genital region, and then the feet. According to Ogas and Gaddam, men are particularly excited by close-ups of many of these areas. Based on research of the site GayTube's top hundred rated videos, eighty-three featured close-up shots of a penis, forty-eight featured a graphic shot of male buttocks, and forty-six featured shots of a male chest. When placing male heterosexual porn and male homosexual porn side by side, there is typically very little difference in what's on-screen other than the gender of the partner. Regardless of sexual orientation, the male brain seeks similar images in pornography. An installation featuring side-by-side monitors of gay and straight porn dramatically showcased this parallel.

Ogas and Gaddam tried to address larger trends and understand why individuals searched for various types of content. For instance, transsexual porn accounts for a relatively high number of searches. Why? Similar to how McDonald's meals satisfy our desires for sweet, salty, and savory all in one, transsexual porn is full of different sexual cues: breasts *and* penises, curvy figures *and* masculine figures. According to some porn insiders, transsexual porn is one of the largest selling niches in all of straight porn.

While a surprise to some—though not to others—many women, independent of orientation, also search out graphic pornography. Several sites look to profit from this information by producing "female friendly" porn. Ogas and Gaddam's research also uncovered a strong female interest in fan fiction, a kind of amateur erotic literature or illustration that centers on erotic scenarios involving pop culture characters. Derivatives of *Harry Potter, Buffy the Vampire Slayer,* and *Star Trek* are all quite popular. And of course, *Fifty Shades of Grey* was originally the result of fan fiction. And we all know how well this particular piece of "mommy porn" resonated with the public.

This data led the neuroscientists to believe women (here the emphasis was on heterosexual women) seem to prefer narrative pornography over visual counterparts. Ogas and Gaddam thus turned their examination to the genre of romance novels. They looked at the ten most common male professions in more than fifteen thousand Harlequin romance stories and found the following to be the most frequent (and likely the most desirable): doctor, cowboy, boss, prince, rancher, knight, surgeon, king, bodyguard, and sheriff. They also found that when searching online romance novels few women used search terms like "huge cock," a prevalent phrase in other kinds of erotic searches. Instead, physical descriptors focus more on details of a man's cheekbones, jaw, brows, shoulder, forehead, waist, and hips. Many scientists attribute attraction to these body parts, which are related to high levels of male testosterone, as a logical byproduct of our biological wiring.

These findings were the starting point for the exhibition, but as always, we wanted to bring in a diversity of voices. That's when I reached out to Arianne Cohen, a woman who had amassed a collection of fifteen hundred sex diaries. Here, separate from scientific perspectives, all orientations and identities would have an opportunity to speak for themselves.

Arianne is a six-foot-two Harvard grad who wrote a weekly "Sex Diaries" column for *New York Magazine* based on the submissions of real people. She published a compilation of these sex diaries in a book called *The Sex Diaries Project: What We're Saying About What We're Doing.*

I'd been talking to Arianne for a few years about how to get her project into the museum, and this seemed like the perfect opportunity. I felt a real kinship with her. Both members of the tribe of "sex workers," Arianne and I had dealt with many similar misconceptions around our choice of careers. Together, we created listening stations where patrons could pick up a selection of red phones and listen to excerpts from the anonymous sex diaries. This feature was a huge voyeuristic hit.

To promote the exhibit, I went on *Huffington Post Live* with Ogi Ogas, who was introduced as "the Kinsey of the Internet age." It would be one of my first on-air interviews since becoming a mom.

While pregnant, I had appeared on *The Today Show* as an expert on breasts, graced *The New York Times* in a photo for my burlesque exhibition, and promoted an appearance for a segment

I did on the Discovery Channel (subject—vibrators) just two weeks before going into labor. One day, I would tell Kai he had been along for the journey in utero. But it had been months since I had done something like this, and I was nervous that my "baby brain," caused by hormones and exhaustion, might take over. I was also worried that, as a new mom, I may have lost some of my proficiency for porn.

I needn't have worried. After a round of hair and makeup, making me feel more and more like my old prebaby self (as a new mom I was lucky to get a swipe of mascara), I felt my confidence return. It was now or never to get back on the saddle, summon a decade of experience, take a deep breath, and talk porn.

The show's host, Ricky Camilleri, opened the discussion by posing the idea that people are probably most open about their sexuality when they are at their computers alone. Sex surveys were nothing new (remember Kinsey), but they relied on participants to truthfully relay information to researchers. And that left the question of how science factored in embarrassment, social stigma, and simple boasting. Are we the most authentic versions of ourselves when we sit in front of our computers alone? Is this when we ask the questions we can't say out loud, when we look for the fantasies we share with no one else? In many ways, this is exactly what Ogas and Gaddam's research was trying to access, and why it was so groundbreaking.

When Camilleri asked viewers to respond to the question, "What would your search history say about your sexual desires?" the first Twitter response that came back was: "Too much."

This "too much," we quickly learned, does not evaporate with an erased browser history. I've spent much of my career sorting through and hunting down the physical artifacts of sexuality, but the reality is that these objects are becoming increasingly digital. Sex collectors and sex collections are evolving before our very eyes. When's the last time you bought porn on DVD? The sex curator of the future will need to perform a sort of digital archaeology to find their artifacts: viral videos, screen captures, and the sexual faux pas rampant on social media. And nothing is ever truly gone from the Internet.

To bring this example to life we exhibited the text from Anthony Weiner's Twitter scandal in the exhibition.

When he decided to run for mayor of New York a year later, its presence in *Universe of Desire* didn't escape the media's attention. With one little artifact and an exhibition focused on sex and the Internet, I became a go-to voice for interviews on porn addiction and how porn affects relationships.

As the Weiner example should forever remind us, regardless of status or position, text, e-mails, and social media postings can, do, and will serve as records of our sex lives for future generations. After this exhibition, I realized that my children would be raised in a world of omnipresent social media and that part of the sex education I needed to teach them would acknowledge that truth.

As I sat in the TV studio, engaged in conversation with the diverse group of panelists—Ogi, Ben Tao (cofounder of ExtraLunchMoney.com, a site that makes personalized porn), Jincey Lumpkin (HuffPost sex columnist and chief sexy officer of Juicy Pink Box)—I saw how opinions gelled and, at times, became heated. What's more, I realized how significantly an exhibition could contribute to discourse, even beyond the walls of a museum. *Universe of Desire* proved to be an exhibition right on the pulse of modern popular culture.

→◆ ◆←

My next opportunity to be on the intersection of sex history and popular culture took place when I was six months pregnant with my second child. Showtime was on the cusp of premiering their new drama *Masters of Sex,* which introduced the sex researchers William Masters and Virginia Johnson to the mainstream. In collaboration, Showtime and *The New Yorker* invited me to L.A. for a screening and to introduce the pilot episode to a group of special guests invited to a downtown Los Angeles theater. My short talk was meant to discuss the history of Masters and Johnson and the incredible impact their work has had on the field of sex research as context for the show. As I rose to the applause of the excited crowd, walking to the front of the theater with my giant pregnant belly ahead of me, I realized I was standing in this position exactly because of people like Masters and Johnson. They had paved the way for me. They had made this decade of one of the most unusual careers possible. It wasn't a stretch to wonder: Would the Museum of Sex even exist if it hadn't been for Masters and Johnson, as well as the long line of brave colleagues who followed in their footsteps? Their work changed our relationship with the entire subject of sex and sexuality.

Masters and Johnson were about to become household names once more, thanks to Showtime, and I was about to become a mother for a second time. As I stood there, in a spot I never thought I would stand, I felt grateful for my opportunity to contribute to the field, in my own little way. That the exhibitions I make bring education and, at times, entertainment into people's lives.

One day I would be able to tell my daughter, Zia, that she was with me that day in L.A. I hoped she would be proud of her mother's contribution to society's ongoing conversation about sex.

→◆ ◆←

I remember telling my mother when I was fourteen years old that I wanted to wait for marriage to have sex. She had been appalled, which I found perplexing at the time. Now, I appreciate her honesty. She told me that it would be a tremendous disappointment to be sexually incompatible with my life partner. And then, of course, there was the phone call from my grandmother when I got engaged.

In the end, they were both right. This was confirmed with each book I read on sex, each exhibition I curate, collector I interview, and news article I consume. Our sexual knowledge plays a huge role in our lives and in our happiness.

Yet, while there is no topic more fascinating or more complicated, no topic that engages more of our time or brainpower, the sexual misinformation in our culture is staggering. Though we consistently overdose on sexual images, it is still very difficult to find accurate information about sexuality and sexual function (I recently read about a grown man who had just learned where women urinate from, previously having believed it was their anus) or how to properly engage in safe sex (no, two condoms is not better than one). It's no wonder *Fifty Shades of Grey* has outsold *Harry Potter* in the United Kingdom. We crave to expand our sexual horizons.

A decade ago, I stumbled upon a unique opportunity to expand my knowledge and push my comfort zone. For my entire life, I've been attracted to diversity, spending my teens and twenties working out my own mixed-heritage identity—an identity that couldn't exist without people having sex. But the Museum of Sex has really helped me understand the true scope of human diversity, diversity at the deepest, most primal level: sexuality.

This most unusual of jobs at a most unusual of institutions has brought a long list of truly unforgettable characters into my life—from sex researchers, scientists, writers, educators, practitioners, collectors, and entrepreneurs, to artists and activists, and those just extraordinarily excited about sex. As curator of the Museum of Sex I have met them all. And it has been the personalities that I have encountered that make my job special. These individuals are at the heart of why my work has been so fascinating and rewarding. Each of my life's milestones over the past decade—marriage, death and loss, motherhood—has been set against this unique backdrop, alongside these fascinating people. In my mind, the personal and professional are intertwined; each informs the experience of the other.

As I've grown, so has Dan Gluck's ambitious experiment. What began as an indie venture in 2002, interested in challenging and transforming people's perceptions of the traditional museum, is now a thriving institution that hosts nearly 200,000 visitors a year. The Museum of Sex is one of the most visited destinations in New York City.

When I sat down to write this book, to try to make sense of it all, Jason had this to say:

"Sex is the Force."

As the only human being in the world not to have seen *Star*

Wars (should I even be admitting this?), this reference was lost on me. So one night when I couldn't sleep, ideas racing in my head, I turned to Wikipedia, which stated: "The Force is a binding, metaphysical, and ubiquitous power." Jason was absolutely right.

Sex *is* the "force" because it is ever present and all encompassing, and it binds everyone across the world, regardless of race, religion, ethnicity, language, class, orientation, gender, or any other category that defines and divides people. Even those who don't have sex are wrapped in it. The history of humanity—what we do, how we do it, where we do it, and how we think—simply can't be separated from the history of sex.

All of the information I have gathered as curator of the Museum of Sex shows that there is a great divide between what we are taught, what we talk about openly, and what we actually want and do.

As chaotic as my childhood was at times, I am thankful that my mother always made sure that sex was an open, honest topic of conversation. Although I didn't always appreciate it at the time, everything I've learned in this past decade at the museum underscores how valuable a sex education really is.

So as it becomes age appropriate, I will provide my children with accurate information about sex and their bodies, rather than waiting for them to be misinformed by someone's older sibling on the playground. And beyond feeling comfortable in their own skin, I want them to find balance between their hearts and minds, as I've had to in my own journey. I want them to live passionately. I want them to find partners who are their best friends, with whom they can share every part of themselves. I want them to understand that sex is many, many things. And as they grow and mature old enough for the words in this book, I want them to have love affairs of their own. I hope the thing they learn most from me is that sex is something you engage with both mentally and physically, and if you communicate openly about it, you can have amazing experiences.

After all these years at the Museum of Sex, the most valuable thing I have learned is the importance of knowing your desires—and being brave enough to communicate them to whoever is lucky enough to share the experience with you.

Although not necessarily what was expected of me as a "curator of sex," my own personal desires were for love, family, and stability—far more banal and tragically heteronormative than what I was exposed to through my work at the Museum of Sex. But that's the thing about desires: everyone has their own, and when it comes to relationships and sex (what we like, who we do it with, how we think of it), each of us has our own take. But regardless of what your desires might be, I have learned across this unforgettable decade how important it is to be honest and true to yourself.

Knowing yourself really is the most potent aphrodisiac you could ever hope to find.

Acknowledgments

I had always heard that a book was like an author's baby. Written primarily between the birth of my son and daughter, this book was by far the hardest, longest, and trickiest of my deliveries. It would have been nearly impossible without my support system of family, friends, editors, and colleagues. Thank you all for making one of my bucket list aspirations a reality. As a lifetime lover of learning, the nerdy girl in me can't quite believe my name actually graces the cover of this book.

Anthropology birthed my fascination with the world around me, a passion I credit to my late professors Harold Juli and John W. Burton, but it was my tenure at the Museum of Sex that ignited it. Thank you to everyone at the Museum of Sex for making this unexpected journey a possibility. For more than a decade you have been my quirky second family. In particular, Mark, Jim, Lizzie, Jess, and Leti, you have been like sisters and big brothers. We have spent years sharing in the most NSFW conversations imaginable, and you each have seen me grow and evolve both professionally and personally. When I first started so many years ago, I never could have predicted the major milestones of my young adult life would occur with the Museum of Sex as the backdrop.

When I set out to write a book about all that I had learned, one of the hardest aspects was trying to distinguish where my academic learning ended and my personal learning began. An interwoven investigation, I oscillated between creating an academic tome to a deeply personal reminiscence, quite the leap for an inherently private individual. While I knew the final work would need to be a synthesis of the two perspectives, it took a wide group of people to help me find my authentic voice and "story." Thank you to my agents, Adam Chromy and Jason Allen Ashlock, for getting my foot through the publishing door. Jamie Brenner and Suzanna Filip, you listened to my life story and helped direct it into a work that felt like me. Through this process, and because of your warmth, you both know more about me than some of my closest confidants. Jamie, thank you, in particular, for being able to "see" my real story buried in all the sex research. Brenda Copeland and Laura Chasen, thank you for not only making magic happen through those critical last drafts but also for your long-held commitment to this book.

My deepest gratitude to my family and friends. Karen Jacobs (Mom): We have been through so much, yet your dedication to my goals and dreams has been unshakable. Your belief in me has been the fuel to my confidence in my abilities and a true gift from a mother to a daughter. Roberta Schnabel (Grandma Duck): You have always been the heart of my creativity. Thank you for inspiring me to be an intellectually curious individual (and for sharing all your statement jewelry with me). And to the loved ones who look down on me: Marvin Schnabel, Elena Escobedo, and William Escobedo. Each of you contributed to the woman I am today. To my "hermanas" and my "mamas," you are my laughter and my sanity. You are the family I was not born with but have chosen, and I am honored you have chosen me right back. Cristina Nardone, there is not a bone in my body that doesn't know your spirit watches over me.

And to my everything, Jason Forbes, my Forbedo. You are my life's adventure. You are late nights, mischief of every shape and size, as well as my true love. And as you vowed on the day we got married, our life together would and never has been boring. I love you madly. We are so deeply blessed that our crazy, at times illogical, love has brought Kai and Zia into the world. Kai and Zia, you are Mama's greatest accomplishment. A little girl from the mountains of Arizona could only have dreamed of the family we have created.